WAITING
gracefully

Praise for *"Waiting Gracefully"*

"*Waiting Gracefully* is not merely a book but a specially scripted memoir of a woman of faith who waited gracefully. Being a part of the writing journey with my beloved friend and sister, Bunmi Oduah, for this extraordinary book makes it all the more beautiful for me!

Written with heartfelt love, great wisdom and lived insights into the ways of God, I believe you're holding in your hands a truly powerful manual for navigating your waiting season with grace, patience and joy. I love this book because the author's insights are so profound, yet so practical, in a way that empowers you to take transformative action.

Get ready to make new stunning discoveries about yourself. Understand the unique seasons of your life, how to make the most of them, as well as define the preparations that make you ready for marriage. You will absolutely love the conversations on detours and reroutes, as they help you heal from disappointments and receive the miracle coming. You are deserving of a love story written by God's hands, and that's what this book is about! *Waiting Gracefully* is a scripturally balanced and well-rounded resource for healing, waiting, becoming and loving in the most empowering ways possible! I pray your life will bear proof of the extravagant love of God, and you will enjoy the Supernatural Marriage He has for you."

*- **Debola Deji-Kurunmi***
(Transformational Catalyst and Founder/CEO)
Immerse Coaching Company

"You were real in this book. You admitted that your journey to marriage was less than perfect, which is something a lot of women can relate to, and you made me see that God's grace is not for perfection; it is for the person we are meant to be. I love how you wove stories of your own experiences/mistakes and the experiences of others into the book to be able to drive the points across. I also like the book style, which is like a friend chatting to another friend."

*- **Olusola David-Elegbede***
(Child Natural Haircare Consultant and Coach)

"This is an inspiring read that is not only self-help but also a reference for everyone waiting to be married. Moreover, I like the practicality of the book. It describes in detail how to navigate the waiting season and offers tested strategies for those who are waiting. These steps, I observe, can be applied to every kind of waiting season."

*- **Chiugo Nwangwu***
(Business Development Manager)

"I love how detailed the content of the book is. I strongly feel a teenager can pick up this book, and it will speak to them. It is not complicated, and it is well thought out, especially the anecdotes in the storyline. It is quite relatable. I could also perceive Bunmi's passion for empowering single Christian women to find themselves and wait gracefully till their purpose marriage season arrives. It is a book that will be suitable for not just Christians, but people of different faiths."

- *Abidemi Taiwo*
(Recruiter)

"Vulnerability, Authenticity, God Factor and Practicality. Bunmi poured her heart into her writing, and the energy screamed, I give you the audacity to wait gracefully, utilize the process of your waiting. Your marriage results season by season will speak for you."

- *Oreoluwa Musa*
(Entrepreneur)

"This is a very uplifting book which every Godly single lady should read. The book breaks down how to build a relationship with God in practical terms to help you in your waiting season and increase your chances of picking the right life partner. Bunmi is very candid about her personal experience and uses very relatable examples."

- *Tolu Shonibare*
(Healthcare Professional)

"The Holy Spirit is all over this book! Bunmi has not shied away from making herself vulnerable to help others. She has been open, honest, obedient, insightful and has oozed confidence, or should I say *Godfidence*, that this book is the heartbeat of God for such a time as this. She has kept it real. The experiences that Bunmi has gone through have allowed her to be authentic and not theoretical, which is so needed in today's society."

- *Igho Mowoe*
(Civil Servant)

"I love how real the book is, the practical examples, biblical references and examples, and the level of vulnerability Bunmi showed in sharing her own experiences."

- *Jennifer Obasuyi*
(Human Resources Consultant)

WAITING gracefully

BUNMI ODUAH

Syncterface Media
London
www.syncterfacemedia.com

Scripture quotations are taken from the King James Version, New King James Version, New International Version, New Living Translation, Amplified Bible, Classic Edition, The Passion Translation and The Message. Used by permission.

No part of this book may be reproduced or transmitted in any form or by any means, graphic, electronic, or mechanical, including photocopying, recording, taping or by any information storage or retrieval system, without permission in writing from the author.

Waiting Gracefully
Enjoying the Journey from Single to Married

ISBN: 978-1-912896-29-5
Copyright © December 2022

Bunmi Oduah
All Rights Reserved

Published in the United Kingdom by

Syncterface Media, London

Cover design by
SimplySumfink

This book is printed on acid-free paper

*I dedicate this book to
every single woman who chooses to embrace
her God-ordained journey to marriage.
May she be you and you be her.*

Contents

Acknowledgements ..*xi*

Foreword ..*xv*

Introduction ..*xvi*

1. Times and Seasons ..*2*
2. Life at The Four Seasons Hotel ..*18*
3. The Qualifying Script ..*30*
4. The Process ..*46*
5. Contracts and Covenants ..*60*
6. Groundwork ..*72*
7. Relationship Building Blocks ..*88*
8. Detours and Reroutes (Part I) ..*106*
9. Detours and Reroutes (Part II) ..*122*
10. The Compass ..*140*
11. Wife in Waiting ..*162*
12. A Kingdom Partnership ..*186*
13. From Promise to Manifestation ..*206*

About the Author ..*225*

Acknowledgements

They say it takes a village to raise a child. Well, this child was raised by a village and I would love to acknowledge them. I would not be here nor would this book be in your hands today if they didn't support me.

My darling Amaechi, thank you for being a promise fulfilled to me by God. Thank you for being the Lapidoth to my Deborah, letting me shine as I am meant to. Your support and encouragement have been second to none. I am the woman I am today because you have been the husband I needed. I love you.

My Arabella and Noah; your hugs and kisses with the words "Mama" make up for the tough days and nights of writing and working. I love you my precious ones.

To my mum, Olusimbo Aboaba. Thank you for everything you have done for me and my sisters. Your love is unrivalled and I am very grateful to have you as my mother.

To my mother-in-love, Catherine Barber. There would be no Amaechi without you. He is the husband I need because of the mother you are to him and me. Thank you for loving me as your own.

To my sisters, May Oduah, Olusola David-Elegbede, Afisurugbola Aboaba and Oyinlolu Sunmoni. Thank you for the gift of sisterhood, laughter and my adopted babies. Your words of encouragement and support have gone a long way in helping me be a better sister.

My cousins, Captain Wal and Aunty Ada. Thank you for providing a safe space for me to spend what would have been lonely holidays as a single woman. Thank you for your words that turned my heart to Christ even more.

To my darling Abike Abu, who would drop anything in a heartbeat if I called. Thank you for loving me and helping me transition into Mrs Oduah. Your counsel has been invaluable.

To my boo, Oluyemisi Vese, the one my husband calls my other husband. Words sometimes fail me in how God blessed me with the gift of your friendship, sisterhood and love. Thank you for the ones people know of and the ones even I am unaware of. I love you my darling bestie.

To my baby girl, Tolu Michaels. You have been the gift that keeps giving, and I can't write my story without you. I want to say thank you for every word, idea, brainstorming session, coaching program, digital course, midnight chat, and most of all, prayer.

To my midwife, sister and coach, Debola Deji-Kurunmi. I will always be grateful for the simple instruction God gave me, "Go to DDK, she will help you." From that first coaching session to this point, you have pushed, prayed and moved me into destiny. *Waiting Gracefully* wouldn't be here without your support, love and prayers. Thank you.

To my Dadee, Pastor Bajo Akisanya. Thank you for stepping into the shoes of a father to me at a time when I needed it most. Your love, care and prayers have moulded me into the woman I am today and I am grateful. Your marriage to Aunty Chizor showed me that marriage is a beautiful institution. Thank you.

To my Pastor, Pastor Agu Irukwu. Your passion for marriages sparked something in me that led to *Waiting Gracefully*. Your marriage to Aunty Sola showed me what was possible. For every word and sermon preached, that kept stirring my heart for God, I want to say thank you.

To my darling Pastor Funke Adeaga, I want to say thank you. For always giving me a space to share what God has put in me and encouraging me. For the messages that came amid discouragement, thank you.

To my mentor and friend, Keji Aofiyebi. The one I run to when I am at a loss. Thank you for always pointing me back to the heart of the matter; prayer and the Holy Spirit. Thank you for supporting me on my marital journey as I support others on theirs.

To my big sister and friend, Abe Jawando. Thank you for always reminding me that what I do is about the Kingdom of God. Your words at the start of this journey pushed me to open my social media page and write my first post. Thank you.

To my sister and friend, Pastor Kemi Olutunbi. Your heart for me and mine especially in these past few years have reminded me that Abba is mindful of me. Thank you for every prayer and encouraging phone call, that comes when I need it.

To my dearest sister and prophet, Teni Giwa-Osagie. Thank you for never holding back what the Father needed me to hear and know. Thank you for beautifying me in so many ways.

To my dear Moyosore Ayeni, my fellow word lover and author. Thank you for sitting across from me as we both wrote. Thank you for supporting me to bring *Waiting Gracefully* Book to life.

To my darling Remi Makanjuola and Dembi Anthony-Williams. Thank you for being my safe space, where I could let down my hair and cry if needed. I want to thank you for constantly reminding me that I am good at what I do.

To my sister-friends; Azeezat Erogbogbo, Oyinade Johnson, Seyi Okundonor, Roli Alade and Bukola Oyinloye. The gift of your friendship has helped me navigate both my single and married days. Thank you.

To my Connect Group Family who rallied around me when my family and I needed it most, what can I say but thank you? Your support gave me the freedom to keep writing and working.

To my dear Wura Arowosegbe, Korede Ikugbonmire and Joella Oyeleye who supported me as I gave birth to this vision. For your support in the Unmarried and Rocking It Community and the Intimacy with God course, I want to say thank you.

To my dear Ogaga Johnson, Oreoluwa Musa, the book launch team and my beta readers. Thank you for being so committed to making *Waiting Gracefully* Book a success.

To my clients, students and audience who have allowed me into your life and space, I want to say thank you. You have engaged with my content, teaching and work, using it to become who God needs you to be. Thank you.

To my friend and brother, Lanre Iroche. Thank you for capturing the vision of *Waiting Gracefully* on this book cover. For also being God's man that I can point others to, I say thank you.

To my editor and publisher, Akin Olunloyo. Thank you! Thank you for walking this clueless girl on the journey of publishing. For your time, resources and prayers over this book, I say thank you.

Finally, and most importantly, I want to say thank You to God, my Father, the One who gave me life. I would not be here today without You Daddy. For giving Your Son, Jesus Christ for me and giving me Your Holy Spirit, I want to say thank You. Thank You for thinking of me as a worthy vessel to bring *Waiting Gracefully* into this world. I am humbled and thankful. Thank You. May I always bring You glory all my days.

Foreword

This book is a must-have if you desire to get married and have a Godly marriage, a marriage God would have you have. In a time when trusting God for marriage and remaining faithful to Him as you do is something that our society frowns on, Bunmi shows how with God, you can wait gracefully for a Godly marriage that will honour God and bless you (and your spouse).

In a well-written, easy-to-read book, Bunmi is brutally honest and vulnerable, as she lays bare her experience of rejection, disappointment and heartbreak. She is equally open when she talks about God's grace and mercy.

I love the fact that she acknowledges God's ability to use anyone. Isn't that just like God? To take the person that we humans would right off and use him/her for His glory!

This blueprint on waiting for marriage as a single woman reassures the reader that there is hope in the wait and gives practical tips on how to wait gracefully.

Bunmi speaks from her own experience and encourages the reader to tap into all that God has for her; His love, forgiveness, mercy, and grace to name a few.

Although it is aimed at single women, I believe there are a lot of valuable lessons that everyone could learn from this book.

It is my prayer that every single woman that reads this book will wait gracefully until God gives her her own marriage that glorifies God.

~ **Agu Irukwu**
Senior Pastor
Jesus House for All the Nations

Introduction

Grace

"The power of God reaching down to humanity for humanity's sake."
~ *Bunmi Oduah* ~

Grace is messy, going into the inner recesses, taking apart all that isn't right to make us who God created us to be, the person He sees. That's the grace available to all of us, most especially when we are waiting for God's promise to be fulfilled. This grace is active, not passive. It is much more than unmerited favour as we commonly know it. Grace is powerful, exuding an ability to change even the worst of people into the very best. It never leaves you the same but takes what is ordinary and makes it extraordinary. Grace changes you, not as men define change but as God defines it.

Oh, I love God's definition of change. In the eyes of God, the worst person is still a candidate for grace and the change it can bring. Grace doesn't say, "You aren't at the highest level of change, so you haven't changed." Instead, grace celebrates even the most minor win because each win means you are changing into the person you were born to be. Grace is beautiful like that, and I grasp it daily. I know that I can't make it through each day without it. Some days I think I can, but I am quickly reminded that I can't each time I falter. Grace is always available. It waits in the wings, calling to me in whispers, other times, with a shout.

To be honest, I didn't understand why God would give me this title, especially as I didn't think I had waited with grace. I felt I had messed up and done God a disservice in my years of waiting to get married. When I look at my waiting journey through my own eyes, it is so easy to see that I was a hot mess for a good part of it. Yet God, in His wisdom and with a healthy dose of humour, thought me worthy. Worthy enough to share about waiting for marriage as a Christian woman.

When I started writing down the journey, I first had regrets. I felt there was so much more I could and should have done in my waiting season. Yet, the title, *Waiting Gracefully*, wouldn't budge. So here we are today. I now appreciate that I did wait gracefully. Not because I was perfect but because daily, I was becoming who God made me. That's what the waiting journey is all about; growing and evolving daily to become the woman God made you.

I remember the day a friend mentioned the words that now form the title of this book to me. I had told her that I was dating someone, and we were getting married soon. Her response was, "Wow! Congratulations," and some other words that I don't remember now. But out of everything she said, what stood out for me were the words "you waited gracefully." Even as I wrote this book, all I kept hearing in my spirit was, you did wait gracefully.

Now, let's be clear; I am no saint. I am far from a saint. My nearest and dearest can attest that I often fall short in this walk of grace. My single waiting season had things I did and said that were far from graceful, godly or holy. If I were to use my standards, I did not wait gracefully. Isn't God an epitome of grace? He chose to use an imperfect vessel like me to tell of His amazing grace. He chose me to share His message of what a season of waiting gracefully looks like.

To be honest, I have often wondered why He chose me to share His heart about waiting for marriage. I counted myself out, but He counted me in. I have come to realise that God uses people who aren't perfect to show what He can do; He uses someone others can relate to. I am that someone He wants to use to show you what is possible - waiting as a single Christian woman in a world that doesn't consider God as standard is possible. So, I have chosen to stand confidently and share the valuable lessons God taught me. Not only me but many others who have waited for a kingdom marriage.

Waiting for a kingdom marriage, also known as God's type of marriage, is honourable and right. That is why it is helpful to have a guide, to know what to do while you wait. That is why I have written this book; the book I wish I had when I was waiting to get married. Looking back, I would have avoided the heartaches and needless rabbit holes I travelled down if I did. There's so much I know today that I wish I had known then. And trust me, I'm not the only Christian woman to say that.

No one, including you, my darling sister (and brother, I see you too), should have to do this alone. You shouldn't have to travel down needless paths in pursuit of something God has given us. God always has a blueprint for everything He does. It may not seem like it, but He does. Scriptures make it clear that He is always there to guide us, be it through a word, an instruction or a principle. So, if you want His blueprint on waiting for marriage as a single Christian woman, you are holding it in your hands. I know that is a bold statement to make, but I say so because it is true. I am so convinced of what God placed in my heart, and I have poured it into the pages of this book.

I didn't write this book only to show you how to navigate this season. Yes, you need to know what to do to enjoy this season and use it well. But, I also wrote it to give you hope while you wait. Waiting, especially when it's for a long time, can cause you to lose hope. The wait can seem to go on forever, and you can't see any visible change. Maybe you're wondering if this waiting season will ever end. I can tell you that it can and will as you walk the path God has chosen for you in this season.

As you take in the pages of this book, I pray that the words will give you the hope you need in this season of your life. Remember, so much can happen to you and for you even as you wait for your desired marriage.

WAITING
gracefully

"This waiting season of your life is a gift, handed to you, all wrapped up. The choice to unwrap it is yours."

1
Times and Seasons

"Embrace the current season of your life."
~ *Gabrielle Blair* ~

I met my ex-fiancé at the end of 2005. I had just graduated after my first degree and was at a family function when this guy walked up to me. Apparently, he had noticed me and told his friends that he was going to marry me. We chatted for a while and exchanged numbers. We started speaking the day after and, in time, went on our first date. One date turned to two, then three, and after a while, we developed a relationship. That's when my journey in wanting to be Mrs Bunmi "Somebody" began.

As the months passed, I had all these thoughts about getting married and settling down with him. In my mind, I had dreamed up our future, and I could see myself playing house with him. When he was getting his new flat, he asked me to choose the colours. After all, it was my house to be. That's how much we could see ourselves together. Now, don't ask me whether I had asked God if this was the man for me.

At this point, I only knew how society had dictated relationships to be. It wasn't based on Christianity, just on society in general. As far as we were concerned, we clicked; we had a connection, and we both wanted similar things in life. At least, that's what I thought at the time, and that was enough for us to get married.

There was one fly in our beautiful ointment; my dad! My dad had a rule about marriage in our house. You weren't allowed to get married until you had completed a Master's degree. He believed it would give you an added edge in the jobs market. Oh, there was also the tiny issue of him thinking that my ex was not the man for me. According to my dad, our backgrounds were not compatible, and this would cause issues later on. From the first day I introduced my ex to him, I could tell that my dad was not keen on the relationship. I am from the Yoruba tribe in Nigeria, and my people have a saying that describes what was happening with my dad. It says, *"what an adult sees when they are sitting, a child can't see even if they were standing on top of a tree."*

This was very true in my case, but I toughed it out with my dad. I did the Master's degree and hung on to my relationship. I thought that if I did what my dad wanted, he would warm up to the relationship and let us get married. You might be wondering why I didn't go ahead and get married without my dad's blessing. At least others have done that and gone on to have great marriages, right? Well, true, but I was still of the mindset that I needed to honour my parents, even when it came to choosing a life partner. It was nothing traditional; it just seemed like the right thing to do.

About a year into our relationship, I met Jesus. It was in November 2006, the weekend of my ex's birthday. I planned to spend it with him, but we had an argument. So, I ended up attending a church service and giving my life to Christ. Now that I knew Jesus, I was pretty sure that He could change my dad's heart, so I started praying along those lines. To be clear, I wasn't asking God if my ex was "the right man for me." Instead, my prayer was, "Lord, let my daddy say yes." Although to be fair, being new to the born-again life, I hadn't grasped how things worked.

However, even with all the prayers, we broke up at the beginning of summer 2009. Interestingly, my dad's view of my ex actually started changing. But I had begun to follow the clues God was leaving to get me on His path for my life. I didn't realise they were clues at the time, but as they say, we learn in hindsight. As I look back on my life, I realise that the choices I made were guided by the hand of God. Now it's clear to see that my waiting season started from the beginning of that relationship.

Even though the relationship ended, the desire to get married didn't. Everything in me wanted to be married, and I looked at every guy I met as a potential husband. This didn't help my journey because there was always an expectation that the next guy could be my husband. Honestly, I never thought I would have to wait so long before getting married. I had it all perfectly planned out in my mind; married by twenty-five and done with childbearing by thirty. But somehow, my perfect plan wasn't falling into place. Upon reflection, I realised I was trying to force a season that wasn't yet due. Even the Bible says in Ecclesiastes 3:1, *"To everything there is a season, A time for every purpose under heaven."*

Not knowing this at the time, I kept on struggling and wondering why the right guy hadn't come along. I don't know about you, but going by how I grew up, I didn't have a clue about life working in times and seasons. I looked at life through the chronological lens of calendars and age. So, as far as I was concerned, having finished my first degree and now job hunting, the next step was marriage. That's why it made sense that when my ex-fiancé came along, he would be my future husband.

Now I have a better understanding of how life works. I can confidently tell you that life works in times and seasons. The more I study the word of God and become a student of life, the more I understand this truth. Our lives are broken down into times and seasons. Yet, the Person who orchestrates those times and seasons is God. Two verses that drive this point home are Daniel 2:21 and Acts 1:7. They clearly state that times and seasons are in His hands and under His authority. Yet, even though He is the One who sets up the times and season, how the season turns out is partly down to you. Your response to what He is doing matters.

For a while, after understanding this, I wondered if my waiting season could have been shorter. I genuinely wanted to know if things could have moved along faster. Did I have to wait those almost eleven years to get married? It's a question that I laid before God, and using the scriptures, He helped me realise that I did drag things out. There were times when I could have responded to the promptings and clues He laid out, but I didn't.

Like the children of Israel who walked in the wilderness for forty years instead of forty days, I spent longer than I should have. But, it's an understanding that I did make my peace with. I like to take responsibility for my actions, whether good or bad. Another reason why I made peace with it is that I would not be writing this book if I hadn't experienced the journey. As a friend of mine told me recently, *"You are right on time even if it seems as though you lost time."* The truth is God makes all things, even my mistakes, work together for my good.

I don't know how long you have been waiting to get married. You may even have a hand in why you have waited so long. One thing I do know is that God can change your season in a second. He can use what seemed like a long wait to bless not just you but many others. I am a living testimony that He can.

Your Single Season Has Purpose

There is a truth I want to share with you that can change how this season plays out for you. It's this: This waiting season has a purpose! You are not just whiling away time, waiting for Mr Right to come along and sweep you off your feet. You are here in this season, right now, because there is a purpose in it for you. As you start to open your heart to this truth, your life will begin to change. This change will first be internal, but it will show on the outside in due time.

"When purpose is not known, abuse is inevitable."
~ Myles Munroe ~

One of the worst things that can happen to you in this season is not understanding its purpose. As Myles Munroe famously said, *"when you don't understand the purpose of something, you are likely to abuse it"*. Imagine trying to use a grill pan to wash dishes. You will most likely get frustrated because the grill pan is for grilling, not washing dishes. For many years before I understood how seasons work, I tried everything to change my season. All was to no avail; the season didn't change.

My deliverance came through my younger sister. One day she told me something that changed my mindset about my waiting season. She said, *"there's a lesson you need to learn in this season. Your attitude and prayer should be to learn it quickly so you can move on. If you don't learn it, you will keep repeating things until you get it."* That was an insight I'd never had about seasons.

I had been going round and round in circles when I should have stayed still and asked, "What am I meant to learn? What does God want to do in and through me?" After that conversation with my sister, you can bet I started asking God what I should learn. The last thing I wanted to do was keep repeating this class. Even though my waiting season went on for a *few* more years, I was not fighting tooth and nail to change it. Instead, I actually started enjoying it. This isn't something many unmarried women can say. Many times, when they say, *"I am living my best life"* (the current slang), they aren't living His best life for them. His best life is one they should enjoy even if they aren't married yet.

Reflecting on my journey, I am thankful for the lessons I learned. They were many, but there was also who I needed to become on my journey through that season. I was and am a testimony of being equipped in advance for what I was yet to face. A verse that springs to mind is Exodus 13:17. It says, *"Then it came to pass, when Pharaoh had let the people go, that God did not lead them by way of the land of the Philistines, although that was near; for God said, "Lest perhaps the people change their minds when they see war, and return to Egypt."* God took the children of Israel through a different route for a reason. It was to equip and prepare them for what they would face in their promised land.

When we go through a season, especially a waiting season, God takes us through it for a purpose. What is that purpose? The first and most important purpose is for you to become the woman God wants you to be in this season and the next. That is His biggest agenda for you while you wait. He wants to ensure that when you get what you are waiting for, you can cope and not wreck it.

Imagine if the children of Israel had not been trained to fight before they got to their promised land? On seeing the armies that wanted to conquer them, they would have turned tail and run. But instead, the Bible says that the fear of the Israelites filled the hearts of the people. Why? Because of the time they spent in the wilderness, taking the route He had designed for them.

The you that God wants to unveil is first being refined internally. A big part of that refinement has to do with your character, the woman you really are. No one likes to hear that their character needs work. Most of us believe we are good people; thus, our character is okay. Well, let me burst that bubble: We all need character development! Even with a good character, remember that there is always room for improvement, to go from good to great. If you think your character doesn't need work, then that very thought alone means it does.

A wise person knows they are a work in progress and have not reached perfection. Many of us think we are wise, but I know that I am nowhere near where God wants me to be. My biggest desire is for more. Even as I write this book, I am going through another waiting season in my life. Once again, I am asking who God wants me to become in this season. The questions you should ask yourself now are, "Who does God want me to become?" and "How do I improve my character?" If you know the answer to these questions, good on you. But if you don't, hope is not lost. Ask Him; He will show and tell you. I will talk a bit more about character later, so even if you still feel stuck, don't worry; I've got you covered.

This waiting season is not only a time to become the woman God created you to be. It is also a time to find out God's purpose for your life if you don't already know it. We live in a time where everyone wants to know their purpose, which is excellent. As noble as this search may be, I can tell you that your purpose is not lost. It's not some item waiting at the end of the rainbow, like a pot of gold. Your purpose is within you, waiting to be revealed to you by God. God's purpose for you is to do His will. Jesus helps us see this in John 4 verse 34 when He said, *"My food is to do the will of Him who sent Me, and to finish His work."* That purpose may express itself in tech, healthcare, teaching, preaching or singing. The key thing is to remember that it is about doing His will, not yours.

At this juncture, I am going to say something you may not like. Your purpose in life is not marriage. But being married to the one God has chosen for you will help you step further into your purpose. I know this for a fact. Ever heard the phrase, "behind every successful man is a woman?" Well, the same applies to women too. Behind every successful, purposeful woman is a man of purpose.

When it comes to discovering your purpose, the easiest way to get started is to ask. Ask the Person who created you for His purpose. Your life's purpose isn't found in a book, podcast, or seminar. You know it by spending time asking the One who created you. Pay attention to the clues He gives you. Note the circumstances that create a hunger for change in your heart. I am not saying that you can't gain insights about your purpose from books or seminars. Of course, you can, but the final answer rests within you and in conversations with your Creator.

If you know your life's purpose, then this season is when you start walking and living it. Don't say, "I'll wait till I get married."

Marriage comes with its own challenges and pressure. You may not believe it but living a life of purpose is a tad easier when you're not married. Knowing what you were born to do actually helps you identify who you will marry. It helps you recognise who can partner with you in fulfilling God's purpose for your life.

If you are already living a life of purpose, remember there's a deeper dimension. There's always more. So, find it. In this single season, God wants you to be His hands and feet in a practical way. This could be by establishing businesses or writing government policies. It could be by researching or producing ground-breaking scientific innovations. But how will you know if you don't dig deeper? Now, more than ever before, you are needed. Governments, social media, technology, communities, and even the Body of Christ need you. They are crying out for change agents because there is such a need out there. You may think that is only for some special people. Well, I want you to know that you are one of those special people. So get up and get going.

I hope you now see how this single season you are running away from can birth something bigger. It is more than just catering for your personal needs and desires. But, how will that happen? By seeking out the purpose of this time in waiting. Purpose matters. Please don't waste your single season running when you can use it to achieve something life-changing. Every season has a purpose, and this season in your life is no different.

Finally, before I move on to the next chapter, I want to address two questions that are often asked. The first is, "What happens when God is silent?" and the second is, "What do I do when the wait seems so long?"

The Silent Season
There will be times during this waiting season when it seems as though God is silent. You pray, fast, ask questions, and it feels like

all you get in return is radio silence. Some have described this as a silent season. Even though this supposed silence makes you feel alone and abandoned, I want you to know this; God is ALWAYS with you. It may not feel like it, but He is. Also, we live by faith and not by our feelings. Our feelings are a good sensor, but they are a poor roadmap for determining God's presence. God says He will never leave you nor forsake you *(Hebrews 13:5b - AMPC)*, and that is the truth. Just because you can't feel Him doesn't change the infallible truth in His word.

Let me tell you a story to help you understand this a bit more. Jacob is on a journey in Genesis chapter twenty-eight and gets to a certain place called Luz. He stays there all night and, whilst sleeping, has a dream. In the dream, Jacob sees a ladder on the earth reaching the heavens. He sees the angels of God ascending and descending on it. God then tells him that He will fulfil the promise He made to his forefathers. God reiterates the covenant He made with Abraham, Jacob's grandfather. He goes on to reassure Jacob that He will keep him wherever he goes. He tells him that He will not leave him until He has done what He has promised.

In verse sixteen, Jacob wakes up and says, *"Surely the Lord is in this place and I did not know it."* God had to speak to Jacob in his dream for Jacob to realise that God was with him. So you see, you are never alone. God is always with you. Even though you can't feel God doesn't mean He's not there. Not only is God with you, but His angels are also with you, waiting to do the bidding of His Word in your life. I once heard from Kris Vallotton that *"when God is silent, He is forming you through His process"*. Kris went on to say that *"God creates through two ways; His Words and His Process."* He finished off by saying, *"the greater work He is doing is done in the silence."* I will talk about God's process later on but for now, be at peace. He is with you.

He may be silent, but He has not left you. He is with you, and though you may not always realise it, He is speaking to you in various ways. You are not alone. I feel like I need to repeat that because it is a truth that will keep you going, especially on those tough days. Remember, God wants to reveal Himself to you in this silent season. So stay encouraged. You are not alone.

The Long Wait

If someone had told me when dating my ex-fiancé in 2005 that I would be single in 2015, I would have rejected it on the spot. I would have kept my distance from them. How dare they try to put a jinx on me. I was sure I would get married at twenty-five and have had my children by the age of thirty. I had it all planned out in my mind, and I seemed to be on track at one point.

Well, I finally walked down the aisle in April 2016. That is almost eleven years after dating for marriage, or so I thought at the time. Eleven years of "God, what is going on? Why am I still single? Why didn't it work with this person? What am I doing wrong? Are you angry with me? Are you punishing me for my past sins? Am I not pretty enough? Why is she the one getting married and not me?" These were some of the questions I asked. I'm sure you have probably asked some of these too, in some form or another. You may not even have voiced them out loud, but they have been thoughts in your heart. It's okay. Welcome to the club.

No one starts their adult life expecting to wait for ages for anything. Correct me if I am wrong but do you start the year saying to yourself, "this is the year I plan to wait?" or "I don't even mind waiting till next year?" I don't think so. No one wants or likes to wait. As members of the microwave generation, we want what we want now, not tomorrow, but today. We do not like waiting for anything. It's one of the reasons why we have VIP queues at concerts and First Class sections at airports. Concert organisers and airlines know that as long as we can afford it, we would rather pay extra than wait.

Waiting is not a word that is synonymous with my generation. So when we find ourselves in a waiting season, we are always searching for the quickest way out. I know I was. I tried all I could to change my season. In some cases, I lowered my standards so that I could move on. God didn't let me off the hook that easily, though. Let's say I wasn't a happy camper.

Sometimes, it may seem like time is stretching out in front of you, almost like a gaping hole that you can't see the end of. Fear grips your heart on occasion as the horizon looks bleaker with each passing day. The thought that God has abandoned you becomes ever so real. It looks like your prayers have gone unanswered, and your steps of faith have yielded no fruit. You bought your wedding dress because you were sure it would be this year, but now it's December, and there's no man in sight. Or maybe, like me, you have bought the household items you plan to take to your husband's house. Okay, don't laugh, but I had heard about a lady who did something similar, and it worked for her. So, why shouldn't it work for me?

It has been two years since you stepped out in faith, and still, nothing has changed. People are beginning to mock this godly path you've chosen to follow. In fact, some have said to your face, "where is your God?" Everyone around you seems to be an expert on finding a man and thinks it's their job to offer advice. Family functions are difficult to attend. You know the topic of your singleness is bound to pop up. Every conversation with your mum leaves the marriage halo hanging over your head. Then there's that aunty. You know the one I am talking about. The one who lacks tact and has something to say about you being single. She likes reminding you that you're no longer a spring chicken. She also keeps comparing you to other young(er) married ladies. That's the one I am talking about.

There are those who should know better who disrespect you. Some young lady who would usually look up to you is being rude to you because of the ring on her finger. In some cases, that young lady might even be your sibling or your younger sibling's wife. You know they wouldn't dare act the same if you were married, but unfortunately, you aren't yet. Everything seems to be about marriage. So much so that your achievements in other areas of your life pale into insignificance.

Knowing that God is the King of all creation and He can do anything, it's sometimes hard not to ask questions. Why is He letting this happen to you? Why won't He do something? The Bible is full of the miraculous, yet it feels like the miraculous doesn't exist when it comes to you. So many people tell of their miraculous marriages. Yet here you are, unmarried and still waiting. Time just seems to drag on. Each day merges into the next. Some days, you are hopeful and expectant. On others, it is hard to put on a brave face, especially when you find yourself in certain places where your singleness is obvious. You want to hide in a hole. You never thought this would be your story, but it is.

I get it. Years of waiting gave me insights I didn't know I would ever get. I had all sorts of emotions during those years, from joy to sadness, despair and frustration. Disappointment, excitement, resignation, acceptance; you name it, I felt it at some point. Some days, a fear that I would be single forever would grip my heart. I had single older friends and family members, and I sometimes wondered if my story would be like theirs. In a nutshell, it was exhausting.

As I mentioned earlier, I had given my life to Christ when I was dating my ex-fiancé, so I was convinced I deserved to be given a husband by God. I had drunk from the cool-aid fountain of *"I am now born again, so life should be perfect."* Apart from that, I also served in a church, prayed, fasted and did all the right spiritual things, so surely I deserved to be rewarded with a husband. If I am honest, I laugh even as I write this because I can see entitlement written all over that thought process. If only it worked that way. Life in the kingdom of God is so different. Yes, we are on the victorious side when we become born again but don't forget that we have an enemy who is constantly throwing spanners in the works of our lives. Plus, all we receive is given to us by grace, not because we ticked some man-made checkbox to get into God's good books.

So, what do you do when this journey stretches on and on? Do you just resign yourself to fate, as some would say? How do you stay hopeful amid what looks like a hopeless situation? I would love to say that there is a magic wand you can wave that will shorten your waiting season, but God isn't a magician. Personally, I think we start with God and end with God. After all, He sees the end from the beginning, so it pays to stay with Him.

Talk to Him. Tell Him what's on your mind. He knows, but He still wants to hear you. Talking also helps you acknowledge what you may be running away from. Do you know some people won't face the reality that they are in a waiting season? They keep saying it is not their portion and speaking flowery Christianese. Don't get me wrong. I have no issue with positive confession, but please don't bury your head in the sand. There is nothing wrong with acknowledging where you find yourself. That you are on a journey you never thought would take this long. Remember, prayer is communication with God, so pray. Pray and ask for strength for the journey. Ask for what you should be doing in this season, so your idle mind doesn't become the devil's workshop.

Don't lose hope. One of the scriptures I held on to while I was waiting was Psalm 119:49-50. It says, *"Remember the word to Your servant, Upon which You have caused me to hope. This is my comfort in my affliction, For Your word has given me life."* I had no one else to hope in but God. Only He could end this long season. I reminded Him of His promises about marriage and the fact that He said He would answer if I asked. I wasn't letting go until He blessed me with my marriage. Another reason why you shouldn't lose hope and give up is that you are closer to your marriage than you ever were. Think about it; you've been at this long, so why not hold on?

Even though you haven't reached your destination, you are not where you used to be. No one starts a journey and stops halfway. You don't want to stop on the highway to your destination, do you? It's not your house, and it doesn't offer any creature comforts. So, don't stop. Don't lose hope. Don't give up. Keep going. Keep believing. Keep trusting and stay in God's word. It is easy to lose faith when you are not spending time in God's word. I look back on my journey, and I know without a shadow of a doubt that the word of God kept me. It played a key role when the journey stretched out before me. It was my energiser for the lonely and tiring days. You may also want to reduce your time with those who reinforce despondency on this journey. Misery loves company, and you don't want to stay with those who won't lift your spirits. Instead, surround yourself with hopeful, faithful people.

Another thing I want to point out is that God has a master plan for your life, and your journey to marriage is part of it. Let me tell you how I know this. Once Adam and Eve sinned, God set in motion a rescue plan. He started talking about Jesus in Genesis chapter 3, yet, Jesus didn't show up till Matthew in the New Testament. According to some research I did, it was a length of about four thousand years (stick with me, I am going somewhere). During those four thousand years, people prophesied about the coming Messiah. People had hopes and dreams. There were even prophecies about what would happen before the Messiah arrived on the scene. Some of the prophecies in Malachi 3:1, 4:5 and Isaiah 40:3 spoke about a forerunner to Jesus.

Then, along came this good, righteous couple. They wanted to have a son, but they were getting on in years. I get the feeling they may have lost hope during this time and thought it wasn't going to happen for them. But, one day! Oh, I get excited when I type the phrase, "one day." One day, while the man was going about his business, he encountered an angel. That man was Zechariah and his wife, Elizabeth. After that encounter, they became the parents of John the Baptist.

I'm telling this story so you can see that God's plan is such that there is a date and time to everything. John the Baptist had been spoken about years before Jesus was born. He was part of God's master plan. There was a set time for his birth because he would be part of Jesus' lineage and announcement. He could not have been born a day earlier or later. John the Baptist was born at the right time.

Your marriage and its time of manifestation have a place in God's master plan. I want to encourage you to view it like that. Even though the wait may seem long, you can stay hopeful and expectant. As much as you may want it to happen today, it won't happen a day earlier or later than its place in God's master plan.

So, what do you do with yourself? I'll show you in the next chapter.

Reflections

What did I already know that was affirmed in this chapter?

....

What new thing did I learn from this chapter?

....

What can I do with what I now know?

....

What example(s), if any, resonated with me and what didn't?

....

What have I learned that I can start doing right away?

....

Actions

Here are three things I will do based on what I learned in this chapter:

1..

....

2..

....

3..

....

2
Life at the Four Seasons Hotel

*"The seasons are what a symphony ought to be:
four perfect movements in harmony with each other."*
~ Arthur Rubinstein ~

Many years ago, some lady friends and I held regular meetings. We would gather to share the scriptures, encourage each other, and prophesy. Those were awesome times; they reminded me of what the early church must have looked like. We met in each other's homes, sharing the Word of God, praying and singing songs to the Lord. We all experienced extraordinary encounters with God during those meetings.

During one of those meetings, I got a new understanding of seasons, mine in particular. While we reflected on the seasons we had been through, I realised what had happened to me when I wasn't married. I kept saying, "I now see what that season was all about." At this point, I had been married for a couple of years and was growing deeper in my walk of God's purpose for my life.

Before then, I had some revelation of what God had been doing in me as a person during my journey. But on this occasion, it became crystal clear. God had been taking me through what seemed like a tough time to prepare me for what I do today. As much as I hated it at the time, I needed to go through that season so I would become the woman God had destined me to be. Now I am grateful for that season of my life, and I would not trade it for anything. It takes a heart of understanding to say that. I pray that God grants you an understanding of your season so that, like me, you can say,

"I see what this season is all about."

There was a particular time when I was struggling to understand what was happening to me. I had been living alone in Brighton, East Sussex at the time but wanted to move to London. I thought my lot in life would improve if I did. The challenge was that I didn't have a job there yet. So, I decided to apply for a role in my organisation based in the London office with the hope that this would help me move closer to London. I scoured through the internal jobs board and found one that looked good and paid more. After some internal tussle on whether I had all the requirements for the role, I applied. Imagine my excitement when I got called for an interview. This had to mean God wanted me to move to London, right?

I went for the interview and, according to the interviewer, did pretty well. Someone with a bit more experience edged me out, though. The interviewer was encouraging. His feedback boosted my confidence in my skills at that time. Yet, that was not enough to soothe the pain I felt at not getting the job. I had already started dreaming of renting my place in London and jumping on the Tube to work. To crown it all, a car thief crashed into my car that week. I parked my car outside my flat, and it ended up wrecked as he tried to escape from the police.

Talk about a week from hell. I was down. I didn't get the job, and now I had car issues to sort out. And as if that wasn't enough, I was also struggling financially. So even claiming on my car insurance was an added expense that I didn't need. One morning on my way to the office, I had a conversation with God. My mornings to work were usually spent praying and praising God in my car. That day was different. As we talked, I laid my pain of wanting to move from Brighton before Him. Now, it wasn't that I hadn't mentioned it before, but this time I did not hold back.

As I poured out my heart to Him, He showed me a colleague

in my mind's eye. It was a bit random, but being in a growing relationship with God, I asked what He was trying to say. What He said next floored me, but it also changed how I viewed my season going forward. God told me that I couldn't walk away yet because the colleague He had shown me was not in a good place. He went on to say that my assignment was to support her through the season she was going through. Once she was strong enough, I would be free to leave. What?! I was in shock, especially as I had never seen how our lives were intertwined in that way. Isn't it amazing how intentional God is about each of us? He is willing to put one person in another's life for a season to help them through.

It makes me think of the song *"Reckless Love"* by Cory Asbury. One part says, *"Oh the overwhelming, never-ending, reckless love of God, oh it chases me down, fights till I'm found, leaves the ninety-nine."* Imagine that. He'll leave the ninety-nine, all for you. That's what He was doing for this colleague of mine. He was in pursuit of her, and I was the vessel He was using. It was a humbling revelation. From that day on, rather than grumble about my situation, I actively partnered with God to show her His love.

Now, imagine if I didn't have that revelation of what was happening in my season. I would have thought what I was going through was all about me. I've already shared with you that this waiting season has a purpose. You must embrace that purpose wholeheartedly with both hands. It is the only way you can walk through it gracefully. Grace, that empowerment to do, is given to us for a reason; to be empowered for the journey ahead.

Seasons are important. Understanding each season you find yourself in will help you make it through with purpose and grace. Even nature shows us that we need the four seasons for our ecosystem to function as it should. For example, certain animals would find it hard to survive if they didn't hibernate in winter. That's why in the run-up to winter, they store food as fat so they can last through the hibernation period. If these seasons are critical to our ecosystem, then the seasons of our lives are essential to our growth.

Each of the four natural seasons has a purpose; if we didn't have them, life as we know it wouldn't exist. Like the four natural seasons, I believe there are sub-seasons when you're waiting. There are ways to tell what the sub-seasons are and what you should be doing. I want to share with you what these sub-seasons are and what they look like. When you know this, you will be on your way to becoming the woman and wife that God wants you to be. As I explain them, I want you to honestly review your life and identify which sub-season you're in. When you do, make up your mind to engage with the season, doing what you need to maximise it and reap the benefits. Believe me, there are benefits in each season, no matter how they look.

Think of it as a Four Seasons Hotel, and no, this is not linked to the real-life Four Seasons Hotel. The hotel has different levels named according to the four natural seasons. You have a different experience on each level, and to go up the lift, you'll need to complete each experience. If you try to jump into the next experience too quickly, you'll soon realise that you shouldn't have. You will most likely head back to the previous experience. That's what life at the Four Seasons Hotel is like. To enjoy the experience, don't rush. Be patient and take your time. Bask in all that happens on each level so that your move to the next will be seamless and timely.

Winter

Winter, winter, winter. Winter is not my favourite season of the year, and I can say with certainty that it is not my husband's either. With the clocks going back at the end of October, I can hear him groaning about the dark and cold weather. Ever since I have known him, he has told me how he would happily move to a warm location until winter is over. Who knows, God may grant his wishes one of these days and give us the capacity to do that.

In winter, the days are shorter, and the temperature is freezing. We have to wear many layers indoors and outdoors. Loads of people don't like winter, and I suppose it is understandable, considering how cold and dark it is. I have always wondered why God would put such a time in the cycles of seasons. I mean, why can't we have long warm days like in summer or fresh sweet mornings like in spring? Why place such a time of barren trees, cold and darkness in the middle of the seasons? Is there a purpose to it? Could it be because it is a time to step back and spend more time with Him? Maybe a season of recharging?

Winter is the time for us to plan for the seasons to come. We certainly spend a lot of time indoors during winter. I know some people love the outdoors, but even they acknowledge that it is not business as usual in winter. They wrap up pretty well to enjoy the outdoors. Coming out without doing so is risking hypothermia and frostbite. I imagine we risk the same when we come out prematurely from the winter experience. We risk experiencing pain and hurt that we shouldn't have to.

Think of it as a time to climb into God's lap, curl up and develop intimacy with Him and yourself. It is in these intimate moments that He reveals what the seasons ahead hold for you. As you develop intimacy with Him in winter, He will reveal His plans for your life. He will speak to you about your identity and show you how He wants you to live.

As a singleton, I initially thought my winter season was a punishment from God. But, in time, I realised it was a beautiful invitation from Him. Farmers use the winter to plan for the planting season, so why shouldn't we take a leaf out of their book? Why don't you use your winter season to review where you are and where you are going? What do you need for the seasons ahead? Do you need to heal from experiences and hurts from previous seasons? Are there certain relationships you need to walk away from or interactions you need to reduce? Do you need to work on certain aspects of your character? I'll talk more about how to do this later, but for now, I want you to think about what winter looks like for you. What needs to change? I want you to imagine God soothing your heart with the strokes of His hands as you curl up in His lap, letting Him work in you.

It is easy to feel like nothing is happening because you are in seclusion and hardly bearing any fruit. But don't despair or grow weary. Just relax. As new plants come out in spring, after the cold and darkness of winter, you will also experience your new. Stay thankful. Remember God's faithfulness in the past. Dwell on what He has done and flow with what He is doing in you in this season. It's a good mood booster; trust me, I know. Let Him recharge your spirit and energise you so you are fit for the seasons ahead. Enjoy the experience. The next level awaits.

Spring

As you enjoy the winter experience at the Four Seasons Hotel, it will, at some point, come to an end. Your heart will be in a better place; you'll be more in tune with God and yourself. He would have given you more clarity on His purpose for your life and shown you the path you need to follow. It's one of the best things about winter. You emerge refreshed and renewed. This is something that makes you glow, a glow that those around you will find hard to ignore.

The experience on the spring level is more exciting. You can almost sense people's attitudes changing with the turn of the season. There is something refreshing about spring. Could it have to do with the days getting longer and the nights shorter, or that buds and blossoms start to abound? The Bible describes it pretty well in Song of Solomon 2:11-13: *"For lo, the winter is past, the rain is over and gone. The flowers appear on the earth; The time of singing has come, And the voice of the turtledove is heard in our land. The fig tree puts forth her green figs, And the vines with the tender grapes. Give a good smell. Rise up, my love, my fair one, and come away!"*

Spring is a time to step out from the dark days and move forward. It's a time of newness and renewed life. It's a time to draw on the energy and experience you received during your winter season. If you fully embraced your winter experience, God will most likely have given you instructions for how to proceed with your life. He may have told you about habits you need to start, stop or continue doing. Spring is the season to act on those instructions. It's a time to take what you learned in winter and start to apply it. As it is planting season in the natural, it is also time to plant what you gleaned from your winter experience.

With spring comes a renewed sense of purpose and drive. You feel empowered because of the experience you've just had. I would encourage you to run with it but remember not to run ahead of the One who gives you the directions. There's no need to run full speed ahead. Check in with God regularly to confirm what He's told you to do. Ask the Holy Spirit to guide everything you do. Remember those instructions I talked about earlier? Spring is a great time to start, but focus on them one at a time, not all at once. There's nothing more frustrating than trying to do everything you learned in winter all at once. It's a recipe for disaster. Let God guide you; He knows the right ones to invest in and when to do so. As the farmer plants strategically to reap the greatest harvest, you need to do the same. Prioritise what you do at this level to gain the full benefits. Even as you do, enjoy the experience of this season.

Summer

Ah! Summer, summer, summer. The season most people love. Warm weather, garden parties, barbecues, trips to the beach. What is there not to love about summer? For children, it's the perfect season as they get six whole weeks off school. I used to love summer holidays as a kid. It was such a fun time with my sisters, although my dad would try to keep us serious. He planned to keep us on the straight and narrow with some school work. Even now, as an adult, I look forward to the warm sunny days of summer. It is the time when I can go outdoors without wearing many layers. Fruits and leaves abound in summer.

There is an atmosphere of excitement, joy and happiness. Everyone's smiling and laughing. Airports are jam-packed. People are excited to be jetting off to some warm and beautiful place. Even those who are not travelling are planning how to maximise the warm weather. You'll most likely be on a roll when you get to this level. Even the rooms on this level of the Four Seasons Hotel are painted with a brighter, more cheerful colour. You are probably excited to be on this level because you know it will be exciting. You have waited to get here. Now that you are here, it is time to enjoy it.

One of the markers of this level is fruit-bearing. Note that I said fruit-bearing, not harvesting. It's time to water what you planted in spring and uproot any weeds. There will always be the possibility of weeds, so you must pay attention. Weeds are those little things that may look like plants but take away from the seeds you have sown. So, as you bear the fruits of the new habits you planted, you want to check any character flaws cropping up again. Pay attention to anything in and around you that may want to take you back to where you are coming from. Are there relationships you don't want that are now rearing their ugly heads? Did you make some decisions that you are now considering dropping? These and many more are the weeds that can potentially ruin your harvest.

Remember, there are thorns in the beauty of every rose bush, and you need to be careful not to prick yourself. Keep your heart and eyes open. There's a reason why people work but also take holidays in summer. If we do this naturally, then how much more in the spiritual realm? Holidays are to relax and reflect. It's not the same as winter when there is a complete shutdown and hibernation. Think of this as a mini shutdown so you can keep going in autumn, the next season.

There's one last thing I would like to say about this level. In the summer, there is the possibility of hot weather. We can get dehydrated and sunburnt when we stay out in the sun for too long. It's important to remember not to get carried away by doing too much; you will most likely burn out if you do. Think of it as overindulgence, planting too many seeds and wanting too many fruits. As much as it's a time to bear fruit, it is also a time to be still so that you don't overexert yourself. Keep growing but take regular intervals to rest and recharge. The harvest coming is worth it.

Autumn

I love autumn. It is my favourite time of the year, but I usually get weird looks when I tell people. A British Nigerian girl born and raised in Nigeria who loves autumn; sounds a bit strange. I mean, what happened to warm, sunny summer? Don't get me wrong, I love summer, but if I had to pick one of the seasons, it would have to be autumn.

For me, autumn shows the majesty of God as a Master Painter as He mixes the vibrant reds, oranges, browns and yellows, creating the ultimate masterpiece. There's something cosy and warming about the autumn coolness as summer gradually gives way to winter. It is a transition season; at least, that's how I see it. It is a season where the leaves are falling, the weather is turning, and winter's invitation is again on the horizon. On this level at the Four Seasons Hotel, the colours are slightly warmer, just like the natural autumn.

After experiencing all that summer had to offer, you are probably excited to reach this level. Finally, you are about to harvest what you planted and tended in the previous levels. If you have been diligent with what you planted, watered and tended in the earlier seasons, it is harvest time. It is the time to reap the bountiful harvest of what you sowed. By now, your crops should be ripe for harvest. As you start to harvest the fruits of your labour, the thought of everything you went through to get here will fade. The pain, fears and doubts all disappear into thin air as you focus on the joy of the reward.

How rewarding and satisfying it is to plant something and reap the harvest. I don't know about you, but I would be frustrated if I got to the harvest season and there was nothing to show for it. What was the point of planting seeds if there was no harvest to be had? We water and tend to what we sow so we can reap in the harvest season. The Bible encourages us to keep doing good because, in due season, we will reap a harvest *(Galatians 6:9 paraphrased)*. Autumn is that due season. This level of the hotel is where the harvest lies waiting for you.

In my research of old English history, I learnt that harvest time was vital because it meant life or death. With a bountiful harvest, the community would be fed, and they would survive. But, with a meagre harvest, the barren winter months would be tough for the community. The same applies to you and me on this journey called life. If we go through each sub-season as we should, we will harvest all we need to step into the next overarching season.

At this level, you have become the woman that God wanted for this season of your life. That's the most significant part of the harvest. Meeting and marrying the man God has for you is the icing on the cake but the main part of the cake is you. You are a more wholesome, healthy and purposeful woman. You are deeply spiritual and surrendered to God's plan for your life. You are no longer seeking marriage at all costs. Instead, you now have a complete understanding of what marriage means for you as His daughter. Your life is an advertisement of what God can do in a person and how He can transform a woman into a higher version of herself. As you look in the mirror of one of the hotel rooms, you almost don't recognise yourself because you look different. Look at you! The new and improved you! That's what happens when you bask in the experience of all the previous levels. You reap a good and bountiful harvest.

Check Into The Hotel

Life at the Four Seasons Hotel is worth every second. The woman you become while you're in there is the woman God wants you to be. Deciding not to check in to the hotel means you don't want to meet that woman. During this waiting season, I encourage you to check in and experience every level. Open the door to each room and take in the experience. Some rooms may be darker than others. That's okay. It is all part of the experience. You will be glad you did.

At the end of the experience, when you meet the new you, I want you to celebrate. Many will never check in to the Four Seasons Hotel. Thus, they may never experience life to its fullest. Some may check in but not bask in the experience before getting married. Others may rush out prematurely because it was too painful or too labour-intensive for them. But guess what? As the seasons repeat each year, so also will there be Four Seasons Hotels dotted through our lives. Because God is a kind and loving Father, He will give us many opportunities to check into the Four Seasons Hotel. He is that invested in seeing us become who He wants us to be. But don't take that as an excuse to check out early. All I am saying is that God has a way of redeeming our missteps.

Later, I will delve deeper into the different activities that happen at the Four Seasons Hotel. I won't have shown you these insights without giving you the details of the experience. What would be the purpose of that? For now, reflect on the understanding you've gained about the Four Seasons Hotel.

Reflections

What did I already know that was affirmed in this chapter?
....

What new thing did I learn from this chapter?
....

What can I do with what I now know?
....

What example(s), if any, resonated with me and what didn't?
....

What have I learned that I can start doing right away?
....

Actions

Here are three things I will do based on what I learned in this chapter:

1..
....
2..
....
3..
....

3
The Qualifying Script

"This is your world. Shape it or someone else will."
~ Gary Lew ~

Nowhere in my plans for my life did I envision getting married in my thirties. I had it all mapped out in my head from a young age. I would get married by twenty-five and have had my children by thirty. Well, that plan didn't pan out. The closer I got to my thirties, the more I panicked. In my head, viewing my plan for my life, this wasn't supposed to happen to me. So, with this mindset, I viewed every man I met as a potential husband. Never once did I think I should be friends with them. What for? How would that help my desire to get married? I know. It's pretty sad to think like that, but at the time, all I saw were the years going by and me still single. I never got to know any of the men I met for who they were. For me, they were potential husbands. Once they didn't follow through, they were tossed into the pile of "it didn't work."

What also didn't help were the well-meaning people, such as family and friends. Someone always had something to say about my marriage or lack thereof. Some were pretty direct, asking when I would get married. Others used prayer to get their point across. There's nothing like, "by this time next year, you will be in your husband's house," to make you feel pressured. I had many of those and learnt over time to say the obligatory "Amen." I know they meant well, but the truth is, it piled on the pressure.

Then there were the comments from people who didn't know me that well. I remember an experience in church many years ago. I attended a small church at the time, so we all knew each other. We were a mixed bag of families and students as I lived in a student town at the time. Being one of the few who wasn't a student and not married, I stood out like a sore thumb. Being an unmarried single lady wasn't a big deal for me, but I guess for some, it was. Hence the comments and prayers I got. On this particular occasion, we were having a thanksgiving service. As part of the culture in the church, families and individuals would dance from the back of the church to the front. They were bringing their "dance offerings" to God. If you are not used to the African slant to thanksgiving, it is a sight to see. A good one, in case you are wondering.

On this particular occasion, most of the families, made up of couples, had gone ahead of me. I was one of the last few. Beside me was an older gentleman who happened to be studying at the time. He was married, but his family were back home in Nigeria, so he was alone in the UK. Anyways, as we danced forward, he asked where my husband was. Remember, this is a small church, and my being single wasn't hidden. I smiled and said I wasn't married. His next statement was, "look at your mates (pointing to the couples in front of us); you better go and get married." How I continued dancing to the altar, I don't know, but dance I did. I smiled and continued dancing. This was one of many experiences I had as a single woman. You may have had the same too, especially if you are from an African background where marriage is a big deal.

In the African community, they expect you to get married by a certain age, especially as a woman. As far as everyone is concerned, once you are of the age of consent, you should get on with the business of marriage. As the man said, my mates had gotten married, so what was I waiting for? I was an anomaly to him because, like most people, I wasn't a child anymore. I had attained some level of education and had a job, so that should suffice for marriage. Sadly, when it comes to this way of thinking, this gentleman is not in the minority.

This kind of thinking is part and parcel of the society I grew up in. I heard it many times in conversations when I was growing up. At the time, it was being said to my aunties, but as I got on in years, I became one of those aunties. According to society, there is a script or roadmap that our lives should follow from a young age. Unfortunately, this script written for us doesn't consider our individuality, life's purpose or destiny. It goes a little something like this:

Baby → Toddler → Nursery school → Primary school → Secondary school → University → Get a job → Marriage → Babies → Live ever after, but not necessarily happily

Nowhere in this script does it consider God's unique path for your life. God wrote a unique script for you before you were born, which is what you should be living out. With society's set script, which is not like God's, is there any wonder why women feel pressured to get married? In some families, you don't even get the breather of finding a job first. The only job you have is to get married. I have heard stories where women get married because their families consider it a duty. Their daughter's marriage is a means to end their poverty. If I'm touching on a nerve here because you are experiencing something similar, please bear with me. The pressure from your family is a lot. They see you as their deliverer, who must get married and marry a man of certain means so they can be free. First of all, I want to know that I see and hear you. It may feel like no one is listening to you, and the weight of this responsibility is crushing you. Once again, I see you. I hear you.

The second thing I want you to know is that there is always light at the end of the tunnel. No matter how bleak your circumstances look at the moment, the light is there. As with all tunnels, you will need to move in the direction of the light. What is the light? The knowledge that God has a good plan for your life. This script that has been written for you is not the be-all and end-all of your life. Will you have to stick up for yourself a little? Yes, you will, but you must remember that God is with you to help you do His will for your life. I'll talk more about intimacy with God and how that empowers you for the journey to marriage later on. You can have the life you desire that doesn't include bowing to your family's pressure to save them. Jesus is the only Saviour, not you. You are human, and there are no guarantees that the man you marry will want to deliver them from poverty anyway.

Now, let me go back to our well-laid-out script written for us to follow by society or culture. I marvel at how it doesn't take into account that people's lives have unique milestones. Those milestones aren't all physiological. Life is not only about growing up, going to school and getting a job that qualifies you for marriage. I mean, look at even the development of a baby. With its growth and development, there are milestones that a baby should meet. With each month or set of months, there are certain things that child should be doing or be able to do. These are developmental milestones. They vary from child to child, but there is an average across children.

So, for example, a developmental milestone for a baby can be having their first tooth at six months. But one child might get their first tooth at four months and another at thirteen months. Children are different and so are adults. With these milestones, you can track the child's development. You can tell how they can or should be able to cope with certain things at that age. The same applies to life and our desire to marry. As a woman wanting to marry, you should have milestones that you hit on your journey to marriage.

What we think are the right milestones usually come from what society and our families have told us. Society says you are ready to marry once you have reached a certain age. It doesn't matter whether you have acquired the knowledge and skills to be a good wife and mother. So far as you have reached the golden age, which seems to be twenty-five, by the way, you must get married by all means. I have wondered why that is the age that every woman wants to get married. If you know, please tell me. Society has programmed us to think that a certain age is what qualifies us for marriage. It might add physiological development or educational qualifications if you are lucky. In my case, educational qualification was a milestone. I am sure you can think of other things that qualify you for marriage, such as your peers getting married. God help you if your younger siblings start getting married whilst you are still waiting. That's another criterion that society uses, and boy, can they rub it in your face!

The questions I got when my younger sister was getting married show that this is one of society's criteria. "Are you married now?" "Where is your husband?" "Is there anyone on the horizon?" Then there were the looks. People studied me so much that they even looked at the rings I wore at the wedding. They were trying to decipher if any was a wedding ring. One thing I am thankful for was that I had prepared myself in advance for what was coming at the wedding. It meant I took the comments with a lot of grace and smiles. Now, I am not saying this happened overnight. I had four or so months' notice to prepare myself before travelling to Nigeria for the wedding. I prayed not only for myself but for my sister and her husband. There is something that praying and supporting someone else does for you as you wait. It takes your attention off yourself and places it on the other person. I spent four months praying every day for my sister's marriage and wedding. Trust me, it shifted my focus from myself to her.

While society might bandy criteria that look right, I want you to know that they aren't the best. These criteria don't take you into account. They don't think of where you are in your level of maturity or your state of preparedness as a wife and mother. We often rush into marriage thinking I'll know what to do. Things will happen because I have matured in age or have a degree. For example, we believe we will know how to cope when we are pregnant. We assume that we will know how to honour our husbands, be great daughters-in-law or parent well. These things don't happen because you signed a marriage register. If they did, so many people would not be struggling in their marriages today, nor would the divorce rates be so high. Jumping into marriage using only societal or cultural standards can set you up to fail. If you have not put in the work of becoming who you are meant to be, marriage might be a challenge for you.

It's like driving a car without taking lessons, thinking we will automatically know how to drive. We all know that we need lessons in the theory and practice of driving. No one gets behind the steering wheel of a car without gaining some knowledge. You also don't start a journey without checking that you have all you need to reach the final destination. Imagine wanting to travel to another country and not checking you have a passport. Or not making sure you have the necessary authorisations such as visas and vaccines for the trip. Or not packing the appropriate clothing for the country you're travelling to. You catch my drift. Without the required documents for the journey, the airline won't even allow you to check in. Without the right clothing, you can be certain that your stay will be uncomfortable. Using society's script will set you up for failure. That may be the failure to reach your destination or to get there ill-equipped.

You don't get married without first equipping yourself or becoming who God created you to be. It's like doing what I said; getting into a car and expecting to drive it without prior lessons. That's a recipe for failure, or as they say in local Nigerian lingo, an epic fail. Don't let the picture of happiness painted by some make you think that these criteria are suitable. They aren't. Many don't share the pain they are going through in their marriages. Once again, society has programmed them to grin and bear it. That is until the cracks start showing on the outside. Societal standards and even family pressure make for poor bedfellows. If some dared to speak, they would tell you that they wished they hadn't rushed into marriage. They would tell you how they wished they had waited and made a different choice. Love may be blind, but marriage is an eye-opener. To have a thriving kingdom marriage, you'll need more than the script written by the generations before you.

So, if the script handed to us by society is wrong, then what is the correct one? I can tell you that it is a script with basic elements yet tailor-made to you as an individual. Why do I say that? Because the marriage God has for you is tailor-made for you, and its success depends on who you are. You are what I call the Constant Variable Factor (CVF) in the success of your waiting season and marriage. We often think that we are not a determining factor in our waiting season or the success of our marriages. We've been taught that God is the only One who determines how things turn out for us. Yes, to some extent, He is, as He has a master plan for our lives. But the truth is that we are the Constant Variable Factor in how things turn out for us. I recently coined this phrase and would like to explain it before going on.

Constant – a situation that does not change or something that occurs continuously (Oxford dictionary). Since the season is about us, we are the "situation" that does not change.

Variable – able to be changed or adapted (Oxford dictionary). We can change or adapt. It all depends on a variety of things such as knowledge, revelation, attitude, mood, feelings and so on.

Factor - a circumstance, fact, or influence that contributes to a result (Oxford dictionary). We influence the final outcome in this waiting season and our marriage thereafter.

God has a master plan for our lives. That is true, but we, the individuals, can influence how that plan unfolds. Our choices, knowledge base, attitudes etc., can influence how things turn out for us. We determine our results. Many people think God determines how things turn out, but look at what He says in Deuteronomy 30: 15-16 NLT: *"Now listen! Today I am giving you a choice between life and death, between prosperity and disaster. For I command you this day to love the Lord your God and to keep his commands, decrees, and regulations by walking in his ways. If you do this, you will live and multiply, and the Lord your God will bless you and the land you are about to enter and occupy."*

Here, God was saying, I have all you need, but at the end of the day, it is up to you to choose. God has a great plan for your life and marriage, but how that happens lies in the choices and decisions you make. Our choices influence our decisions, and these determine the results we get in life. My hubby has a running joke that further explains this point. He says that a man keeps praying to God to win the lottery. The prayer is constant. One day, after praying the same prayer again, God says, "Okay, you will win the lottery but at least buy a ticket!"

You can pray for a good marriage or for your waiting season to end, but what are you doing about it? Are you taking steps to create the atmosphere or circumstances for God to move? God needs your participation to do what He wants to do for you. It is something I learned that changed my view of how to get answers to my prayers. On this journey to marriage, you are the CVF that determines how things turn out. As you align with God and His plan for your life, you will evolve into the woman for your marriage. God has a tailor-made marriage for you. So I hope you can see that you are an important factor and why using society's standard script won't work.

Since society's and God's scripts aren't the same, how does God's differ? I'll start by saying that His script is unlike any you could craft yourself. God's script has far weightier things than your age or having a job. That's what I realised after being on my waiting journey for some years. To be honest, I wish I had learnt this earlier as I would most likely not have waited as long as I did to get married.

God's script is based on the following criteria:

- Understanding God's definition and purpose of marriage
- Having the right relationship with God
- Knowing your identity and purpose
- Emotional wholeness and maturity
- Repentance or a mindset renewal
- Preparation – becoming a wife before you get married

Understanding God's Definition and Purpose of Marriage

Ask a group of people why they want to get married, and you will get varied answers. You will get answers from "companionship" and "having children." There might be a religious response like, "I want to partner with someone for God's purpose." These are some of the answers I got when I asked this question on social media. Some want to get married so they don't feel guilty when they have sex. Others want someone to share the bills with. For some, it is because they believe they are ready for marriage. For others, it is the next thing to do in their life's journey. We all have our reasons for wanting to get married, and everyone who wants to get married does.

Whatever your reason, this is the question you should be asking. "Why should God give me the marriage I desire, and what are His definition and purpose for it?" Knowing this will help you determine if you are ready for marriage. In the world today, many consider marriage to be a contract between two parties. Two people with a similar desire, in this case, marriage, come together. If they feel the other person ticks the right boxes for them, then they are good to marry. The challenge with viewing it as a contract is that the parties can choose to part ways if it doesn't work.

To God, marriage is a covenant and one that you shouldn't embark on lightly as it is binding. Walking away isn't that simple. The scars of breaking the covenant usually run deep. I will spend some time in a later chapter talking about what marriage is and isn't. When it is time for you to get married, I want you to make the right choice based on the right knowledge. When you understand marriage and its purpose, you will take your time before getting into it. You will also be more discerning of who you want to go on the journey with. You will know you will be with them till death separates you.

Having the Right Relationship With God

If you want a godly, thriving marriage, then you need to have the right relationship with God. You can't get it outside of Him. Anything you get will be a counterfeit version of the real thing. In this relationship, He reveals your identity, purpose and His plan for your life. As you yield to Him in the relationship, He will guide you in the direction you need to go for your marriage. He has a process He wants to take you through for your marriage. Intimacy with Him, through relationship, makes the process easier.

There is something I have come to realise. It is from Matthew 22:37-40, and it says, *"Jesus said to him, 'you shall love the Lord your God with all your heart, with all your soul and with all your mind.' This is the first and great commandment. And the second is like it: 'you shall love your neighbour as yourself.' On these two commandments hang all the Law and the Prophets."*

When you build a relationship with God, you will live out the truth in this scripture. As you do so, your life will go in the direction He wants. You will grow intimate with yourself, which is so important. This is what will give you the capacity for a great marriage. You will learn more about these in later chapters. For now, let me say that having the right relationship with God will shape everything about your life. Who you marry and the type of marriage you have will be shaped by this relationship. So, I would say that growing this relationship is a worthy investment of your time.

Knowing Your Identity and Purpose

I have a saying when I am teaching about waiting for marriage; "who you are will determine who you marry." I learned this as I waited to get married. It shaped everything for me when it came to making the right choice of a life partner. Your identity, that is, your values, personality and spiritual identity, is who you are. What you were created to do and where you are going is God's purpose and vision for your life. These three, identity, purpose and vision, determine how you live out each day.

Identity, purpose and vision also make you more discerning when it comes to marriage. When you know who you are and where you are going, you can shut your ears to the pressure to get married. You can also ensure that you don't settle with the wrong person. Here's an example I use a lot that gives single women clarity about this. If you know you are meant to be working in the business world, you won't settle with someone who wants a housewife. The two paths don't align. This understanding changed the game for me.

I reached a certain point on my journey, especially as I hit my thirties, where I became more confident. My confidence didn't grow because I now had a man. No, ma'am. My confidence came from knowing my identity and purpose and who could live with that. When well-intentioned family members and friends tried to hook me up, I was clear on whether to say yes or no. It also meant that not every man who said hello to me benefited by receiving my phone number or unlimited access to my time. I wasn't being proud or arrogant. I had become more self-aware and focused on what I wanted and where I was going.

Emotional Wholeness and Maturity

We all have emotional baggage, some more so than others. Our baggage could be from how we grew up or the trauma we experienced in our past. It could be from the experiences we have been through at various stages in our lives. If you have lived on this earth, you will have some emotional baggage. A piece of baggage that can catch us out while we are waiting to get married is our relationships, and I don't just mean relationships with the opposite sex. Our relationship with our parents, or the lack of it, lumbers us with baggage. Then add in betrayals from friendships and friction in work relationships, and you can see how easily we accumulate emotional baggage. By the way, did you notice that I haven't mentioned failed relationships yet? With those whom we thought we would experience our happily ever after with, there can be baggage.

When you don't deal with your baggage, you're setting yourself up for failure or future pain. Even the best relationships can turn out badly where there is baggage if care isn't taken. You can have all the makings of a good marriage, and it still ends or limps along. Why? Because your emotional baggage can give you a fractured lens to look through. It is why you could be with the one God wants you to be with and still have the worst time. It isn't that he isn't the one, but your baggage and lack of maturity are getting in the way. God's desire is for you to heal and be whole in your emotions so you can thrive in your marriage.

Repentance or A Mindset Renewal

I'll never forget when I understood what repentance was. It was a light bulb moment for me. I had been in coaching for some months when my coach mentioned the word repentance. My mind immediately went to a sorrowful reflection that I'd done wrong and the desire to change. She said it wasn't only to be sorrowful in the heart. It was to have a renewed mind or a change of mind about the thing you did wrong. Wow! I had never seen it like that. So why am I sharing this insight with you? I am doing so because "as he thinks in his heart (mind), so is he" *(Proverbs 23:7a)*.

If you have the right mindset about men and marriage, you will likely attract the right man to yourself. You will also experience the type of marriage God wants for you. The same is also true if you have the wrong mindset about marriage. If your mindset does not align with God's on marriage and the qualities of a good man, you're not helping yourself. You won't have the marriage He desires for you. I am not trying to be mean or a Debbie Downer; I'm just telling you the truth. Your mindset, the contents of your mind, are like a magnet that attracts things to you, good or bad. If the contents are good, you will attract good and vice versa. We often think things happen to us, but the truth is what happens to us is a result of what is in our minds. I know this may seem outlandish, but I will break it down later in the book. So, keep reading.

Preparation – Becoming a Wife Before You Get Married

If there is one area that society tries to help us with on the journey to marriage, it is this one. Right from when we are girls, we are being prepared for marriage. Think about it for a second. If you grew up in an African home, you likely learned how to cook and keep a home. Even if you didn't grow up in an African home, you might have learned how to care for your home. You were asked to help with chores and all. As you grew older, your responsibilities increased at home. You may have heard you would have your own home one day and must know how to look after it. Don't tell me you didn't have that experience.

Even if you didn't, as you got older, you must have started to see and hear that a wise woman keeps her home. I don't know about you, but no one went into the finer details of what it meant to me. If you were lucky, and they did explain, it was usually tied to the "you must be a superwoman in your home" script. Don't know what that means? It means you must do everything for your husband and children. At the same time, you must ensure that nothing goes wrong in your home. The Proverbs 31 woman, bless her, has been used as the standard for the perfect wife. She is the ultimate superwoman. Yet, what no one points out is the fact that she had maidservants. Has that ever crossed your mind?

Society will try to condition how you must prepare for your marriage. However, I want you to know that the other points I listed earlier will help prepare you for your marriage if done properly. Are there other things you should do? Yes, there are. You should read books, take courses, grow your social skills and even save money. These are all good things that prepare you for your marriage. But please remember that your preparation is first internal, then external.

His Ways Are Not Society's Ways

As you can see, God's script with His criteria is very different to society's ideal script. His thoughts and ways are far higher than ours. What He focuses on in deciding when you are ready for marriage is not the same as what society focuses on. Did you notice that none of the things I shared focused on your age, degree or job? That is because the things that qualify you for marriage are first internal. The external things like your age and job matter, but they aren't the most important. When you focus on them and ignore the internal, they become a plaster covering what you haven't dealt with.

You may say, "But Bunmi, others have gone ahead and gotten married without doing the things you've listed. Why should I?" First, you may not know if they did the things I listed. Not everyone goes into the specifics of their journey with you. Second, their circumstances may have forced them to do what they didn't do before marriage. Third, this is not about them but you. This is about your marriage, not theirs.

This recent conversation I had with someone will help you understand what I am saying. She said, "I wish I had done whatever you did because it is clear from your marriage that you did it right." Her words touched me, and she was right. She was in a challenging marriage and was realising some of the things I mentioned earlier. She not only acknowledged that I had gotten married the right way. She also made it clear that she would not have married her husband if she had known better. The fruit of the transformation I experienced in my years of waiting was showing in my marriage. I didn't particularly like what was happening when I was going through my waiting season. Now that I am married, I am so grateful for the experiences I had.

That is why I am encouraging you to go through the process God has for you on your journey to marriage. All you are experiencing in this season is not a waste of your time. It will yield results many years down the line. Society's script isn't the standard for your marriage. It is not the best way to determine when you should get married or who you should marry. I will talk about who you should marry later on in the book. By now, you must have an inkling that I won't be talking about whether he is tall, dark or handsome. Those are admirable characteristics, but they don't make for a godly man or great marriage.

There is no shortcut to a great marriage, and anyone who tells you otherwise is not being kind to you. A great marriage, one that beats the statistics of divorce, honours God. It creates an environment for raising godly children. That kind of marriage starts with the process you go through in your waiting seasons. I will cover that as we delve further into this book. Also, during the course of this book, I will go deeper into the criteria of God's script. I will help you see what He is doing with you this season. You will learn how to align with Him so that this waiting season equips you for your marriage. You will start with the process God takes every single one of us through as we wait. Then, when you understand what is happening, you will embrace the process and let it do its job in your life.

Reflections

What did I already know that was affirmed in this chapter?

....

What new thing did I learn from this chapter?

....

What can I do with what I now know?

....

What example(s), if any, resonated with me and what didn't?

....

What have I learned that I can start doing right away?

....

Actions

Here are three things I will do based on what I learned in this chapter:

1...
....
2...
....
3...
....

4
The Process

"I pray with great faith for you, because I'm fully convinced that the One who began this glorious work in you will faithfully continue the process of maturing you and will put his finishing touches to it until the unveiling of our Lord Jesus Christ!"
~ *Philippians 1:6 (TPT)* ~

In life, there is a process to everything. Nothing happens by accident. One thought that has weighed heavily on my heart recently is why there are so many unmarried women. I get a lot of messages from single women, primarily through social media. When I go out, I see many unmarried women who want to get married. I've wondered why this is so. I know the answers aren't in the statistics peddled in society or online. It's deeper than more women choosing to focus on their careers these days or more women than men in the world. That myth isn't true. Check the world population statistics, and you will see that the ratio of men to women is roughly equal.

Those are facts, but they aren't the truth. Truth is what God says about a matter, and I was in search of truth. So, I went to The Truth, God Himself. Being very solution-driven, I knew that if anyone had insight on this matter and how to solve it, it was Him. So, as I started laying my heart's burden before Him, it felt like He beamed light into my mind. I was coming from the angle that there is more for singles today than there has ever been. I may be wrong, but it seems like something is happening for singles everywhere you look. So, with so much "support" out there, how come people weren't getting married? Why were there so many unmarried people around, especially those who wanted to get married? Why did an increasing number of people quit within the first few years of marriage?

The light He beamed into my mind as I asked these questions, focused on one word: PROCESS.

As I pondered that word, He started to help me see what He meant. In life, most things come in seed form. To get the best of the seed, it must mature and grow into a plant and then a tree that bears fruit. The seed goes through a process, from seed to tree. It doesn't become a tree, shrub, or even a plant overnight. Some things have to happen for it to change and become what it needs to be. The same applies to the journey to marriage and all other aspects of life, for that matter. Since my focus in this book is unmarried ladies, let me stay with our subject matter.

When the desire for marriage hits, whether from external pressure or an internal knowing, you receive it in seed form. You have all the potential for marriage in you, but it is still wrapped up and untapped. Let us call it untapped potential. Now, here's where things go awry. At this stage, based on societal, cultural or familial norms, we think that desire is all we need. Since we desire it, all we need to do is to step into it, right? But, if you are in the body of Christ, things go a step further. You hear that if you pray, fast, and sow a seed towards your marriage, it will happen. Now, these things are not bad, and I don't want you to think they are. They make things happen for us and to us. Yet, there are so many other things that need to happen on the journey that I will go into later. It is these misconceptions that have caused so many ladies to still be single.

Going back to my seed analogy for a moment, here's what I want you to know. Prayer, fasting and other spiritual activities help unlock the untapped potential within the seed. They are part of the process the seed needs to go through to become a tree, but they aren't the entirety of the process. Let me tell you about a more significant part of the process. It is called maturation.

Depending on how you grew up, there is some level of conditioning and dysfunction at your seed stage. Now, let me pause and say, "I am not saying you are dysfunctional." Please hear me on this. We all received some level of dysfunctional programming from our upbringing. We were raised by imperfect people. Whether we like it or not, they likely have passed on some or all their imperfections to us. Those imperfections then form the beliefs and perspectives through which we experience life. That is what I am saying here. If we never pause, reflect and aim to grow, we can end up with these imperfections playing a significant role in who we become.

Without a disruption from God, we may never pause in this race called life. By the way, disruptions are God's way of getting our attention. Without them, we run through life, following the standards and traditions of men. We check and define ourselves by those standards and hope we meet up. So, when the desire for marriage hits, the same thing happens. We look at how society has said the trajectory of our lives should go. As I already said, we use man-made prescriptions for how we should make it happen. God's intention wasn't for us to do it like this. He wanted us to receive the desire of marriage, turn to Him and let Him mature us into the people ready for it. The version of us that received the desire for marriage (version seed) is not the version that will step into the marriage (version plant). And it most certainly isn't the version that will be in the marriage ten or thirty years down the line (version tree). The difference between version seed, plant and tree is the process of maturation. For all of us, there is a process of maturation we need to go through to be able to step into the desire or blessing we seek. To not embrace our process is to choose not to receive the desire we have or receive a substandard version of it.

That's the truth and The Truth Himself was the One who opened my eyes to see this. He said blessing people with marriage was a simple thing for Him, but His hands were tied. So many people weren't the versions they needed to be to step into the marriage they desired. God isn't a wicked father who gives His children what will hurt them. He would rather keep them in their single state till they were fit to handle their marriage. No parent puts their child behind the wheel of a car without first giving them lessons. They also ensure they have a licence to drive the car. God said to me that the same applies to moving from being single to being married.

As He opened my eyes to this realisation, my next thoughts were, "What is the process?" I immediately wanted a solution to the problem that was now glaringly obvious. There must be a solution because there was no way God would show something like that and not provide an answer. I was determined to get the answer so I could share it with you.

As I pondered on possible solutions, God took me down memory lane. He showed me my journey and how I matured. The woman I was when the desire for marriage hit wasn't the same woman who married my husband eleven years later. I went through a process that made me good enough so that I could get married and not wreck it. I say this to let you know there will be a process for you to go through if you want to get married. The process doesn't end when you get married. Oh no, it continues as one constant thing in life is growth. On the threshold of marriage, though, God looks at you and sees that you have matured enough for Him to place you in it. Not only will you survive, but you will also have the capacity to thrive.

In the scriptures, this process of maturation is called dying to an old way of life and embracing a new one. You will need to shed the old, including the conditioning and dysfunction I mentioned earlier. You will have to take on a new way of thinking and life. There are many things we have imbibed in our upbringing and other life experiences. These restrict the untapped potential that lies within us. The process aims to strip all that away so that what is within us can grow and bloom. So we can become the version we need to be for our marriage. A scripture that encapsulates this is Exodus 13:17-18 NASB: *"Now when Pharaoh had let the people go, God did not lead them by the way of the land of the Philistines, even though it was near; for God said, "The people might change their minds when they see war and return to Egypt." Hence God led the people around by the way of the wilderness to the Red Sea, and the sons of Israel went up in martial array from the land of Egypt."*

When God takes you through a process, it is because He wants you to be able to get and stay in the blessing you desire. He wants to build your capacity so you can handle what you are believing Him for. That way, you won't turn tail and run at the first sign of trouble. He is willing to take you down paths you would never have chosen for yourself. He knows those paths will take you into the woman He wants you to be.

One thing you must be conscious of is that your path to your desire will be uniquely yours. It won't be like anyone else's. You are a unique woman crafted by God to marry another unique individual. Your marriage to your future husband is a unique marriage that will bring glory to Him. There are some basic spiritual laws and principles that govern you here on earth. How those laws manifest in your life is solely tailored to you. So, even though I will share the principles that apply to every woman on her journey to marriage, how they will apply to you is different to me.

Let me help you understand how each person's process is unique in more detail. This is important, so you don't see someone else's process and despise your own. It happens to all of us; we catch a glimpse of someone else's journey and think something is wrong with ours. What we don't realise is that the process has been crafted with us in mind. It even takes into account our missteps on the journey. You can see this in the lives of Joseph and Moses in the Bible. Both were born with the role of deliverer written into their spiritual DNA. It was what God would have them do at the right time, but the process for each of them to become a deliverer wasn't the same. Joseph was to end up in the palace, and so was Moses, but their path (process) to getting there was very different.

As I read their stories and, like a spectator, watched their journeys, I saw so much. They both had a process of maturation that led them to God's final destination. It is interesting to see, and I want to show you. Let's start first with Joseph's story.

Joseph

At the age of seventeen, Joseph, son of Jacob, gets an insight into his future. In his excitement and naivety, he runs to tell his brothers. Now, being a spectator on the outside looking in, I want to tell him, "Don't do it!" In his flawed way, Jacob, Joseph's dad, had created enmity between the sons of his first and second wife. Jacob's brothers hated his guts because they saw he was "daddy's favourite." Knowing how the story goes, I can see the foolishness of telling his brothers his dreams. He does it not once but twice, including his dad the second time. This drove his brothers mad. Not only did this spoiled little brat get their father's affection, but now he wanted to rule over them. It was a recipe for disaster and a misstep that would take Joseph on a journey he never expected.

That misstep led to his brothers selling him into slavery. As a slave, Joseph is accused of attempted rape and dumped in jail, the key to his cell thrown away. By anyone's standards, this was the worst kind of luck. How do you go from being the special kid to a cell in the king's jail for a crime you didn't even commit? If you are from my part of the world, they'd say your "enemies" have won.

Yet, the story doesn't end there. Joseph stays honourable and God-fearing throughout. He goes on this life journey without a murmur, accepting what has happened; he continues to be himself. At this point of the story, I notice something I don't think I've seen before. A thought crosses my mind. I know it is God giving me an insight into something that isn't explicitly written in the chapters of the Bible.

King Solomon says in Proverbs 22:6, *"Train up a child in the way he should go, and when he is old, he will not depart from it."* Joseph was brought up a certain way as a child. The Bible doesn't explicitly say so, but I want to believe that his closeness to his father meant his father taught him what helped him when he was enslaved. There's no way Joseph could have feared God if he wasn't raised to fear God. Yes, he may have lacked wisdom in some regard, but he had a foundation of faith.

This insight is vital for you and me. People aren't good by accident. They are usually trained to be good and godly by someone who has authority over them. In most cases, that is a parent or guardian. But, some do so by training themselves. Good character and ethical and moral values are also training-based. And I don't mean classroom-type training. Joseph's process, which started from the day he was born, continued throughout his journey. Let me continue the story. You will gain even more insight into how the process works and prepares you to step into what you desire.

Joseph had all this training as a child that set the stage for the rest of his journey. When he got to Potiphar's house, that training came to bear. So much so that even when Mrs Potiphar, as I call her, tried her luck with him, his training "protected" him. This was a process-defining moment for Joseph.

Seriously, think about it for a moment. If that was a test, Joseph passed with flying colours, by God's standards. By our human standards, not so much. Why? Because he ended up in prison for it. That doesn't sound like a pass; more like a fail. If I were in his shoes, I would think that dream of many years ago was a figment of my imagination. I may even think God hated me. But I am not Joseph and thank God I don't have that kind of mindset anymore. Now, when things don't go according to the plan I have in my mind, I don't think God is against me. Instead, I ask Him what is going on and what I am supposed to do next. It is a mindset shift that has changed my life as a child of God and a part of going through my process with God.

Joseph's process wasn't ideal. It wasn't the path anyone would choose to get to the palace, but in God's eyes, it was all working together for good. If you don't know God's nature, you may think of Him as wicked. Why would He let something like that happen to Joseph despite him doing nothing wrong? But then, think about Joseph's story for a second. God didn't ask his brothers to sell him or tell Joseph to be unwise. All that was their doing, but because God can spin what seems negative into good, He did.

After being in the king's prison for a while, Joseph's training, character and the presence of God worked for him. It caused him to find favour with the prison warden. It's all part of the plan. Joseph has to get into the palace, and now it seems it will be by any means necessary. I know I wouldn't have chosen this path, but hey, who am I, but a spectator turned narrator?

Eventually, we begin to come to the climax of his story when he interprets the dreams of the king's butler and baker. With all the "suffering" Joseph had been through, you would think this is it! The interpretations were spot on. He would be set free and given employment somewhere in the palace. But, alas, it was not to be so. It takes another two years for anything to happen. Two more years in his process, faithfully serving and working where he was.

The process can be tough, but it is rewarding in the long run. At the appointed time, God orchestrates events to ensure that Joseph is the one who can solve the king's problem. In doing so, he receives the highest place of honour in the whole land, second only to the king. He ends up in the palace as God had planned from the beginning of time.

His dreams as a seventeen-year-old boy were a preview of the future. In his immaturity, he misinterpreted them. By the time he was interpreting Pharaoh's dreams, his ability to interpret had improved. He was accurate in his gifting. With his gifting, he delivered not only Egypt, his adopted country, but also the nations all around. And yes, to conclude his story, his brothers did end up bowing before him - the irony.

Moses

Moses was also a deliverer and one destined for the palace. Yet his journey was different to Joseph's. This shows that even though our destinations may seem similar, our paths are unique. Moses' journey to the palace was so different to Joseph's. Moses ended up in the palace in what seemed like the best way possible.

He had been born at a time when Pharaoh hated the children of Israel and maltreated them. Yet, despite all the maltreatment, they continued to grow and prosper. Talk about throwing sand in your enemy's eyes. They already hate your guts and are doing all they can to get rid of you, but you won't go away. Gosh! That must have been so annoying for Pharaoh, so much so that he changed his tactics to murder. He told the midwives to kill all the boys born at the time, but the midwives feared God too much to do so; wise women.

It was in this atmosphere that Moses was born. His mother knowing her child would be great hid him as long as possible until she couldn't anymore. She had to think of a way for him to survive outside of her household because his days were numbered if he stayed. Now, this part in the story always amazes me; the way God orchestrates events to work in His plan. Moses' mother places him in a basket and puts him amongst the reeds of The Nile. Pharaoh's daughter happens to come across him and rescues him. Yes, this is the same Pharaoh that wants all the Israelite boys dead. Not only does she rescue him, but she takes him home and adopts him as her son.

Wait, hold on! What are the chances of that happening? Moses, the deliverer chosen by God before he was born, ends up in the palace just like that. Now, not only is he not killed, the same person who wants him dead is raising him as a prince. A prince! Not a slave but a prince. Wow! When God is taking you through a process, there is nothing He won't do to get you where you need to be.

Let me contain my fascination with God's orchestrations. We continue the story because it doesn't end there. In time, Moses grows up as a prince but doesn't forget his roots. Hey, I doubt the Egyptians would have let him forget even though his adopted mother was the Princess. One day, he is out and about and comes across an Egyptian maltreating an Israelite. The deliverer DNA in him, which is still being "formed," rises. To deliver the Israelites, he kills an Egyptian man. Oh, oh. Bad move.

This gets him into trouble with Pharaoh, and he has no choice but to flee. He escapes to a town called Midian, where he spends the next forty years. During this time, I wonder if it ever crossed Moses' mind that the assignment for his life was to tend sheep. This man was a deliverer, but he had tried to deliver God's people way before he was ready. As a result, he found himself on what seemed like an extended holiday from his assignment. As I pondered this, it became clear that trying to step outside of your process too early will cost you. It cost Moses.

After forty years, God, the one marking this process script, decides that Moses is ready. I have to say, we don't get told much about what happened in those forty years. Yet seeing that God chose to bring him out of exile and send him back to Egypt, something was clear. He was now ready for his God-ordained role.

By the time we see Moses in action with Pharaoh and the children of Israel, something has changed. You can tell he is much wiser than the young, impetuous man who killed an Egyptian man many years prior. Not only was he wiser, but he also understood how the palace worked, an experience no other Israelite had. This was because he grew up there. The new Pharaoh was his adopted brother who he grew up with. So, Moses wasn't intimidated by him.

After some dramatic activities that would make a great movie, Moses delivers the children of Israel from Egypt. They were free after more than four hundred years of slavery. Can you see why he needed to go through a process? He wasn't just saving one person or family from a bad boss. He was saving an entire nation and bringing them into what God had promised them. In God's books, he had to be the right man for the job. The same applies to you. You have to be the right woman for where you are going.

Did he still have flaws? Yes, he did. Moses was human, but by God's standards, he was ready for the assignment. God's process ultimately wants to work on every part of you. Like Moses, you can get to a stage on your journey where you are fit for the assignment. Yet you will still be a work in progress. Remember, God uses willing and available vessels, not perfect ones.

Different Process, Same God
Joseph and Moses' journey to the palace was unique to their assignments. One needed to be trained outside the palace, whilst the other needed to be trained inside the palace. Yet end up in the palace, they both did. You may have compatriots on a similar journey when God takes you through your process. Please resist the urge to compare what is happening with them to what is happening with you. Your journey is uniquely yours even as He prepares you for where He is taking you, in this case, marriage. God wants to work on certain parts of you because He knows who you will marry. So, it is unlikely that He will take you down the same path as your sisters, friends and colleagues.

The process is vital to God. There's nothing He does that doesn't have a process attached to it. As you embrace the process God is taking you through, I can assure you that it will all work out for your good. He doesn't do anything to harm us but to help us and put us in the future He sees in His mind's eye for us. That's what He says in Jeremiah 29:11. It's why I try not to fret when I sense that I am going through a process.

Finally, I want to return to my musings about processes and solutions. If there is a process and we are all supposed to go through it for this thing called marriage, what does it look like? Are there markers or tick boxes I can check to know I am doing it right?

The answer is yes and no. Let me explain. Some general checkboxes will show that you are maturing, but each person's process is unique. Please note that God is the One marking your script. He is the One who will tell you if you are meeting the bar. He is also kind and will show you through various means, especially if you're not in a close, intimate relationship with Him, where He can say it to you directly. So yes, there will be some general tick boxes, but no, it won't be the way mainstream society defines it.

I want you always to remember that the solution to stepping into the desire for marriage is a process. The process matures you into God's version of who you are meant to be so you can step into your marriage and stay in it. As I have considered that word process, I've started to see areas where God expects maturation in us. The thing about this process of maturation is that it usually isn't a walk in the park. That is why so many of us shy away from it. It is painful and sometimes messy, but it is worth it at the end of the day.

As we go further into this book, I will help you understand the key areas where God expects us to mature. I will also show you how He expects us to mature. In pondering the process and its key role in getting you from unmarried to married, I've seen the answers. God has shown me the main areas where He expects His daughters, you included, to mature.

My job now is to show you these areas and how you can go through the process that will give you the marriage you desire. As you embrace your process, God will transform you into the woman that can enter and carry your marriage.

Reflections

What did I already know that was affirmed in this chapter?
....

What new thing did I learn from this chapter?
....

What can I do with what I now know?
....

What example(s), if any, resonated with me and what didn't?
....

What have I learned that I can start doing right away?
....

Actions

Here are three things I will do based on what I learned in this chapter:

1. ....
....
2. ....
....
3. ....
....

5
Contracts and Covenants

"Marriage is by nature a covenant,
not just a private contract that one may cancel at will."
~ *Bruce C. Hafen* ~

When I met my ex-fiancé, I was naïve. I thought I knew what I wanted, but the truth is I didn't know much. Looking back now, I realise how naïve I was. I know knowledge is progressive, but at the time, I was clueless about what I so desperately desired. As far as I was concerned, marriage was about setting up shop with someone and having 2.5 kids. That's what I had learnt about marriage, and it seemed like something I could do. So, I went after it with determination. That's why I didn't mind toughing out with my dad. Even though he was not keen on the relationship and thought we were incompatible. That was the crux of the matter. My dad was sure that even though I wanted to get married, the person I had chosen wasn't the right person for me.

I completely agree with him now, but this girl was in love at the time, and nothing could tell her otherwise. Well, in time, I came to learn that my dad was right. In Yoruba, there is a proverb that says, *"Oun ti agbalagba nri lori ijoko, omode ko le ri lori iduro."* It means "what an elder sees while sitting down; a child can never see it while standing up." At the time, I couldn't see what he saw. Today, I can, and he was right. He knew that compatibility was important in marriage. That is something I have come to learn over the years and teach other women.

In my ignorance, I was sure he was the person for me, and marriage would be a walk in the park. Now, in hindsight, I know we were ill-matched. The marriage would have limped along at best or broken down at worst. Could God have redeemed the marriage? Yes, He could have, but would I know what I know today for Him to be able to do so? Rather than ask God to redeem something I shouldn't have done in the first place, how about I do it His way so He doesn't need to? God can redeem any situation. He is the God of all flesh; nothing is too hard for Him. There's no marriage too far gone for Him to save, no situation too dire for Him to fix and no person too broken that He can't heal. But I've come to know that God would prefer that we follow His ways and path from the onset. So, yes, He could have redeemed the marriage, but I am in a marriage that doesn't need redemption, which is way better.

Since I didn't know much about marriage or understand what it meant in God's books, it seemed disposable. I had it at the back of my mind that there was always a back door if things got tough. I had seen family and friends whose marriages hadn't worked, so I knew I could leave if things weren't working. I am not alone in this thinking. The marriage statistics show that many, including Christians, have the same mindset. Christianity doesn't make you immune from divorce.

It saddens me the number of marriages I know that have broken down. I've had to stop myself from being cynical. This is after I see the number of flamboyant weddings on social media that don't make it past the first two years. It is worrying. In time, I've learnt to say a short prayer when that thought crosses my mind. I ask for the marriage to last, not limp along but flourish as God intends.

It was never God's intention for marriages to break down. But I have realised that they break down for various reasons. In this chapter, I want to focus on one of the main reasons I believe marriages fail. I've already alluded to it, but our view of marriage today is that it is something we can walk away from if it doesn't work.

Remember that I mentioned that I was clueless about marriage? Well, I didn't stay clueless. Over time, I started to grasp what marriage meant. I also learned that a broken marriage comes at a cost to both parties and any children they might have. Don't let people glamourise life after a divorce. It is painful, costly, and takes its toll on the parties involved. Ask anyone who has experienced divorce and separation, and I'm sure they will tell you how painful it is. So, why is divorce so painful and costly? Because it was never part of God's original design. In His original plan, a man and woman would come together and stay together. The way He designed their coming together didn't allow for the parting of ways. I'll talk about that in a bit more detail shortly. For now, as you read this, please know that divorce and separation are painful.

It doesn't help that society then shames those who have been through it. As if they haven't received enough bashing. You hear statements like "divorce is a sin" or "anyone who marries a divorcee commits adultery." It is especially sad when this comes from the lips of fellow Christians. I've had to respond to these statements several times. Here is what I have come to learn from the scriptures about divorce. First, it was not God's design but a concession given to man because of the hardness of man's heart *(See Matthew 19:7)*. In God's original plan, the marriage would last. My view is that if this was His heart, it means He can still do it. He can heal a marriage if both parties let Him. Second, there are certain circumstances when the Bible says, go ahead and get divorced. Now, I'm not saying that is what God wants, but He will give concession in some circumstances.

There are two circumstances that I know of. First, where there is persistent, unrepentant immorality. Second, when an unbelieving partner leaves a believer. In fact, in the second case, Apostle Paul says the believing spouse is free from the marriage. Why? Because God has called us to live in peace. Can you imagine that? God would rather people be at peace than not. Those who make judgmental statements about divorce usually haven't experienced it. Or they don't know God's heart on the matter. There is a reason I share about divorce at this stage. If you meet a divorced person, I don't want you to hold yourself back from experiencing a beautiful marriage. If you don't know what led to the divorce, you can miss out on experiencing a beautiful relationship. If God gives grace, so should you. Remember that we are first people before we are what society labels us. We must let the Holy Spirit guide us in all things, including being with someone who got divorced.

Now that we have settled that let me share what I learned about marriage during my waiting season. Remember, I was clueless but didn't remain so forever. Thank God for that. I came to understand that marriage is a covenant, not a contract. Before I talk about covenants, let me explain a bit about contracts.

What Is A Contract?

A contract is a mutual agreement between two parties with obligations on both parties. We tend to have contracts in our everyday lives. This may be with our employees, contractors or even teachers. We have an agreement with them that they will do their part, and we will do ours. With contracts, there is an expectation for the parties in the contract to perform. It is performance-driven with timescales. There are terms and conditions to meet in the agreement. For example, an employer expects an employee to carry out certain duties. In return, the employer agrees to pay them a salary with employment benefits. If the terms and conditions aren't met, then, as in the case of employment, the employer can let the employee go. Our society also tends to view marriage this way, hence the term marriage contract.

My previous mindset was that marriage was a contract; if I no longer liked the terms, I could break it off, just like my mobile phone contract with my provider. Except it is not that simple. Even breaking a phone contract has cost implications. Depending on the terms, I must settle any outstanding charges on the account. The same applies to breaking off a marriage contract. There is a cost, or I should say, there are consequences to breaking it off. It is why you should not enter into marriage casually. Even these days, with all the empowerment messages on walking away if things don't work, it still isn't that easy.

Having the mindset that marriage is a contract has consequences. Let me share some things that happen when you have this view of marriage.

1. You always have an exit mindset
You may not say so. Yet, your subconscious mind stores this information away. If you weren't aware, the subconscious part of your mind drives your life. It's the part of your mind that you always revert to. You know how you do some things without thinking, like brushing your teeth or taking a bath? Well, it is your subconscious mind that drives those actions. So, when you tell your subconscious mind that marriage is a contract you can break, it stores it. It then uses that information to help your future decision-making. When things get tough in the marriage, it will tell you that you can walk away because that is what you have told it. Walking away then becomes more and more attractive. Why? Because your mind will repeatedly play that script back to you. This leads me to the next point.

2. You will not fight for the relationship
Why would you fight for the relationship when you know you can walk away? What will be your motivation to try and make things work? That's what happens when you view marriage as a contract. It makes you see the marriage as dispensable. There's a way you handle an expensive item that's different from how you treat something cheaper. Picture this; you've just bought a new car, and you saved a lot to buy it. When you get behind the wheel, there's a way you drive the car so that it doesn't get scratched. You don't

want people to eat in the car so that it stays nice and clean, just the way you bought it (taking a dig at my hubby here, hahaha!). Why do you do that? Because you value the car. The same applies to the way we view marriage. Marriage is not dating, and we are not fooling around for the sake of fun. It is much deeper than that, and when you have the right view, you will treat marriage with the respect it deserves. You will fight for it and protect it.

3. You will not make an effort to grow your staying power

You may have heard the description, the microwave generation. It's synonymous with the idea that we want things quickly or right now. Something that you often hear about my generation and those after is that we don't have staying power. People describe us as the ones who walk away if things aren't going our way; the ones who don't stand for nonsense. Now, I am not advocating staying in a bad relationship; far from it. I am saying that when you understand that marriage is not a contract, you will develop staying power. When you view marriage in the right way, your motto will be, *"This marriage will work, or it will work."* There are no other options. When your mind knows there is no back door, it will look for ways to resolve the ongoing issues. It's how your mind works. When presented with a problem, it will look for a solution, which may include walking away. But, when you've told it that walking away is not an option, it will find alternatives for the problem at hand. It is in this process that we build our staying power. The more you do this, the more your mind gets used to finding solutions that help you stay.

4. You don't see the good in the person anymore

When you view the marriage as a contract, with the option to walk away, you stop seeing the good in the other person. It's human nature. You'll see the things that make you want to leave the person rather than what attracted you to them in the first place. Have you ever heard how gratitude can change your perspective of your circumstances? This is a practice usually recommended when people are in counselling or coaching. The same applies here. When you see what is good about them, it changes your outlook on them and the marriage. Unfortunately, the opposite is also true. When all you see are the negative things, it will cloud your perspective of the marriage.

This is by no means an exhaustive list. I am sure you can think of many more ways viewing marriage as a contract can be a recipe for disaster. Because contracts are performance-driven, you will find things the person isn't doing. Or where they aren't performing as they should. As you work your way through their performance or lack thereof, they will keep coming up short. As with the employment example, once they stop meeting the terms and conditions, they have to go.

A Godly Covenant

On the other hand, what is a covenant from God's perspective? Just like a contract, a covenant is also an agreement, and a divine covenant is an agreement between God and man. Marriage was God's idea, and so the covenant between a man and his wife is one backed and witnessed by God. The Bible is full of covenants between God and man. There's Noah, Abraham, and, of course, the one He made with us through Jesus' death and resurrection.

With a covenant, there is a sworn oath to do something, no matter what the other party does. It is not performance-driven but based on the nature of those who cut the covenant. When God cut a covenant with Noah, He instituted it, not Noah. All Noah did was obey, and God said, "I'll do this for you." Obedience opens the door for covenants. God instructed Noah to build the ark and save his family and the creatures. Noah did what he was told, and God established a covenant with him and his descendants. There were no conditions attached to it. The responsibility of fulfilling the covenant was on God. He kept saying, "I will…" I don't recall the

Bible saying, "and Noah said, I will…" You can read the story in Genesis 9. Not only did God establish the covenant between Him and Noah, but also to everyone who came through Noah. This means covenants impact unborn generations, not only the person in it. Take a look at Abraham.

Like Noah, God asked Abraham to bring a sacrifice. When the birds of prey would have attacked the sacrifice, Abraham chased them away. He made sure that what he brought before God was not attacked. In response, after consuming the sacrifice with fire, God made a covenant with Him. The covenant was not just between Abraham and God but also between Abraham's descendants. When you read the scriptures, you see the covenant when God interacts with Isaac. The same happens with Jacob (later known as Israel). That covenant is still running today. Abraham is long gone, but Israel is still thriving because of that covenant. Now that's the power of a covenant.

Here are some things that happen when you view marriage as a covenant.

1. You will be backed and supported by God

God is the author of marriage. It was His idea, and He knows how to keep it. When you go into marriage with God as the third strand in the marriage *(Ecclesiastes 4: 12)*, guess what? You are inviting Him to back you, and when God backs your marriage, it cannot be easily broken. Not only that, but you will also have all His wisdom to deal with the challenges that may arise. He will give you the backing you need to face anything that comes your way in the marriage. He has a vested interest in what He instituted. As He continues to establish what He promised Noah and Abraham, He will do His part in your marriage. When you do marriage with God, you will enjoy His promises.

2. You will be obedient to any instructions

When you know that marriage is a covenant, you will be willing to obey the instructions you receive. It won't matter whether your spouse is playing their part or not; you will do your part. Noah and Abraham reaped benefits from God because they obeyed His instructions. He gave them clear instructions on what He wanted them to do. They went ahead and did it. God responded. My view of marriage being a covenant with God means obeying whatever instructions I receive. Some of the instructions don't make sense, but I do them anyway, and I see the results. A friend of mine told me a story that helps drive this point home.

In this true-life story, a woman was dealing with challenges in her marriage. Her husband was mistreating her and cheating on her. He went as far as bringing another woman into their home. This caused her a lot of pain, as expected. One day, as the lady prayed about the situation, she got some instructions. God asked her to pray for her spouse and treat him kindly. God also told her to pray for her husband's mistress. She did as she was instructed despite the pain she was feeling. To cut a long story short, things broke down between her husband and his mistress. Today, they are happily married. The woman's obedience saved her marriage. Yours will too.

3. You will sacrifice for the marriage

Both Noah and Abraham had to sacrifice. When they received the instructions, they went ahead to do what was needed. In Noah's case, he was mocked by the people around him for building a boat when there was seemingly no need for one. In Abraham's case, he brought the animals for sacrifice and set them up. He then had to drive the birds of prey when they tried to attack the sacrifice. When you view marriage as a covenant, you take a sacrificial attitude towards it. It won't be that your spouse's actions will endear you to sacrifice, but you will see the bigger picture. You will have the prize, a marriage that glorifies God as your goal. Since that is your goal, you will make the necessary sacrifices. Your pride will most likely be your biggest sacrifice. God wants to burn your pride to establish His covenant for your marriage. Don't worry; it will be worth it.

4. You won't walk away
When you view marriage as a covenant, your marriage will be worth fighting for. Not only that, you will develop staying power. I mentioned earlier about how your mind will do what you tell it. When you tell your mind that you are in a covenant, it will believe you. Not only will it believe you, but it will also no longer see walking away as one of the available options. Your mind is now conditioned to understand that walking away doesn't happen in a divine covenant. Now, once again, I am not advocating staying in an abusive marriage. I would never want that for you. Do I believe that God can redeem an abusive marriage? Yes, I do, but only He can give the strategies for resolving the issues in such a marriage. He has wisdom for ALL situations, including abusive marriages. But I know you won't end up in an abusive marriage. You are reading this book and will put what you are learning in place, right?

How You See Matters
It's clear that having the right view of marriage matters a lot. I remember when the change about what marriage was happened to me. It was circa 2009 or so. I had these messages about marriage sent to me by my younger sister. In one of the messages, the preacher talked about having the right view of marriage. Then he spoke of marriage being a covenant. As he described marriage in this way, he used an example of a practice that helped drive home the point. He explained how you would mix salt when you wanted to establish an agreement with someone. You would have your part of salt, and they would have theirs, and the salt of both parties would be mixed together. The agreement could only be

broken if each party could take their salt from the mix. Talk about something impossible. No way can that happen. Even *Numbers 18:19 (AMPC)* describes the covenant of salt as one that cannot be dissolved or violated. That's why you don't walk into marriage casually.

Before you walk into marriage, take time to settle things in your heart. Marriage is a covenant, not a contract. It is not performance-based. Decide with yourself now in your single season, before the decision you will make on your wedding day. Your marriage will work, or it will work. Failure is not an option. Now, go on and settle that in your heart.

Reflections

What did I already know that was affirmed in this chapter?

....

What new thing did I learn from this chapter?

....

What can I do with what I now know?

....

What example(s), if any, resonated with me and what didn't?

....

What have I learned that I can start doing right away?

....

Actions

Here are three things I will do based on what I learned in this chapter:

1..

....

2..

....

3..

....

6

Groundwork

"There is nothing that happens in the physical that has not already been settled in the spiritual."
~ *Olusola David-Elegbede* ~

"I think we should pray," my friend said to me. She continued, "I've seen something in the spirit realm, and we should pray for its manifestation." "What have you seen?" I was curious to know. "That it's time for you to get married. Let's spend some time praying for your marriage to come to pass."

I agreed, and we did. Then I continued with life as I had come to a place where I was learning to trust God to do what He had said. By the way, my friend has a strong prophetic gift. This was not the first time she had given me a prophetic word about my life. I had tested the gift enough to know that this wasn't her flesh speaking. I am saying this because I don't want you to fixate on the wrong details in the conversation. God speaks in diverse ways, and one of them is via prophecy and prophetic words. God had already spoken to me about it being time for me to get married six months prior. My friend didn't know this but spoke as led by the Holy Spirit. It was one more confirmation and further insight into what God had said to me.

About a month later, things started to move along. I discovered that a dashing young man liked me through someone close to me. At this point, I had learned to ask God about many things, and this was no different. I went to God and asked what He thought. His answer was a simple yes; this was the man. He took my mind back to the conversation with my friend the month before. He said this was the manifestation we prayed for. I am married to him today. Some other conversations and circumstances also confirmed this was the man for me.

This is what I want you to know. When it is time for you to get married, you may or may not have the kind of circumstance I just described. Why? Because your scenario would be unique to you based on your relationship with God. Plus, we are two very different individuals. So how things pan out for us in life will be based on who we are and the destiny God has for us.

What helped me in this particular instance was my relationship with God at the time. God spoke to me all the time about other parts of my life. So it wasn't strange for Him to talk to me in this way when my friend called me. I had been growing my relationship with God to the point that Him speaking to me was normal. This is the same thing I tell women when they ask me for help. You should learn to hear God's voice before it is time to make a life-altering decision such as marriage. Why? So, you know it is Him and not your feelings speaking. The chances of getting it wrong due to your feelings or what someone said are lower when you know God. They are also lower when you know how God speaks to you and you hear Him regularly.

Another thing I would say at this point, which I illustrated through my story, is this. What others say God is saying should confirm or affirm what you know or sense to be true. Even if they tell you something out there, a part of you should be able to say, this is God or not. You can always ask the Holy Spirit to confirm or deny it if you are unsure. It's why the Bible says we should test all spirits. Not every "God said" is God said. Some are people wanting the best for you, while others are plain words with no heavenly backing.

Look at me running away with myself, talking about hearing God.

Let me start by saying your relationship with God is the most crucial relationship in your life. It is your most important relationship in life before all others. It is the relationship that affects every other relationship, including with yourself. If you get it right, your other relationships will work. Jesus clearly says so in Matthew 22: 37 – 40. *"Jesus said to him," 'You shall love the Lord your God with all your heart, with all your soul, and with all your mind.' This is the first and great commandment. And the second is similar: 'You shall love your neighbour as yourself.' On these two commandments hang all the Law and the Prophets."*

So if you want every area of your life and relationships to work, you'll want to practice this. First, build a relationship with God, then with yourself and finally with others. By the way, that whole Jesus first, others second, yourself last, otherwise known as joy, doesn't line up with this scripture. Indeed, Jesus comes first, but I can tell you that you cannot pour from an empty cup. If you don't know how to love yourself, you won't know how to love others well. What you will give them will be a dysfunctional version of love, no matter how nice and noble that love looks on the outside.

How will you love yourself? By starting in a love relationship with God. Something beautiful happens when you are in a relationship with God. It is more than attending church and spending quiet time with Him in the morning. It is more than praying for extended lengths of time. These activities are good. But if they are the total of your relationship, then it isn't a relationship. I know it sounds weird to say that but think for a moment. I want you to think about your relationships, especially those close and important to you. Are they based on tick box activities or interactions? To be in a relationship with anyone, God included, is to have a connection with the person. By the way, God is a Person. How do I know this? Because you and I are made in His image and likeness, and since we are people, so is He.

I want you to settle that in your heart. You are building a relationship with God. Not only that, but the relationship is unique because you are a unique person. God isn't looking for clones but children who desire a Father-child relationship with Him. When you read the Bible, this is so clear. How He dealt with one person differs from how He dealt with another. Are there basic laws and principles that we need to follow as His children? Yes, there are. Yet, these don't change the fact that we should be looking to build a relationship with Him. I keep using the word relationship because I want you to know that it is more than a religion or religious activity.

When you build this relationship the way He wants, you will start to see changes in other areas of your life. That is why I want us to settle this relationship with God part first. Everything else I will share in this book is built on it. Think of it as laying the foundation before putting up the building structure we see. If the foundation is good, then the building, which is everything else, will stand the test of time. If the foundation is faulty, you can imagine what that will do to the building. I love how Jesus describes laying the right foundation in Matthew 7: 24-27. *"Therefore whoever hears these sayings of Mine, and does them, I will liken him to a wise man who built his house on the rock: and the rain descended, the floods came, and the winds blew and beat on that house; and it did not fall, for it was founded on the rock. But everyone who hears these sayings of Mine, and does not do them, will be like a foolish man who built his house on the sand: and the rain descended, the floods came, and the winds blew and beat on that house, and it fell. And great was its fall."*

You can get to a place in your life where things go well. Even when life isn't going the way you expect, you won't be a yo-yo. I know this is possible because I am living it, and so are many others. It doesn't mean we don't have down moments, far from it. When those moments or circumstances come, we don't stay there. We get back up and keep moving, one step at a time. Recently, I asked God why I wasn't unstable and constantly fluctuating in my faith and life. His response is an insight that I want you to understand. He said, "because of what you did in your single years." This waiting season is a blessing, and you must view it as such. When I first started this journey to marriage, I didn't view it as a blessing. I just wanted to get out. You may be feeling the same way that I did. There's nothing wrong with that, but I can tell you that God doesn't want you to get out. He wants to build you up in this season so you can handle what comes in the next. Your single season matters. What you do this season has a long-term impact on your future. Don't despise it. Instead, embrace it. It has so much to offer you if you would only embrace it.

There is a tribe in the Bible that I believe will help you understand what I am saying a bit more. They were the sons of Issachar *(1 Chronicles 12:32)*. They understood the signs of the times and knew the best actions to take. They understood the impact of times and seasons. They had also learnt to read the seasons as they evolved and then acted based on that. When I read about them, they intrigued me. They didn't have a prophet telling them what the seasons meant. Instead, they knew what each season meant and did exactly what needed to be done in that season. I wondered why they were like this. As I did, God helped me understand that they had a relationship with Him. Since He is the controller of seasons, He showed them what the seasons meant. God is the one who changes times and seasons *(See Daniel 2:20-21)*. If you truly want to know about times and seasons, He is the best person to show you. Looking at the sons of Issachar, it became clear to me that they were close to the One who controls times and seasons. Think about it like this. How will you know how to use a thing if you don't consult the one who made that thing or has its instructions?

In this waiting season, to fully appreciate it and know what to do, you must be close to the controller of seasons – God. The worst thing you can do in this season is grow spiritually cold or distant from God. It won't serve you any good and will only add to your frustration. Instead, this season is ideal for building your relationship with God. You want to be so close to Him that you can understand everything that is happening to you and around you. I am so grateful for the growth of my relationship with God in my waiting season, and I want you to be too. My life is much better today due to the many days and nights spent in God's presence. Even when I messed up by having sex, my relationship with God put me back on track. Oh yes, I did fall off the purity table on some occasions.

At this point, you may wonder how you grow this relationship with God in a way that matters. Don't worry; that is what I am about to share with you. First, let me lay the foundation so your heart is in the right place to embrace what I am about to share next. You must know that you are building a relationship, so you don't think I am showing you a list of things you need to do. God is more interested in your *being* than your *doing*. That is why you are a human being, not a human doing. Will you have to take action to grow the relationship? Yes, you will, but your actions must come from a place of connection rather than activity. This is important. Having this understanding will change the way you relate to God. He wants you in a place of being with Him rather than doing for Him. The two are not the same. This is a major issue for those of us who grew up in church culture. We learnt that the activities we did define our relationship with God. It is why we throw ourselves into all sorts of church activities. We believe these activities define us as Christians. If there is anything I have learned, it is that God doesn't look at it in the same way.

In God's books, your relationship with Him far outweighs any activity you can do. The heart you have for Him is way more important than the action you do in His name. This does not mean you won't or shouldn't do things for God. Far be it that you think that is what I am saying. What I am saying is this; *relationship, not religion!* Religion says, "do this and do that to earn God's love." Relationship says, "even if you don't do this and that, I still love you." Religion says, "keep the rules if you want to get anything from God." Relationship says, "follow My Spirit and what I am saying, you will get what you desire." A relationship is way easier than religion. It takes a burden off us that we were never meant to carry. So, as you read, I invite you to embrace a relationship with God. It will change how things happen to and for you in this season.

At this point, I trust that there are stirrings in your heart for a relationship with God. So don't worry; I won't hold off any longer sharing how to build a relationship with God.

The Way In

Building a relationship with God starts with Jesus, not growing up in a Christian home, going to church or singing in the choir. They are good things, but they don't bring you to God; Jesus does. It is why He came into the world in human form. When Adam and Eve sinned, having a relationship with God stopped happening. For that relationship to be restored, there had to be a sacrifice of blood. Jesus came, and He did that when He died on the cross. He provided the link to our relationship with God back to us.

We often want a deep relationship with God, but we want it without Jesus. The truth is that it is not possible to do that. Jesus made it pretty clear that "I am the way, the truth and the life. No one comes to the Father except through Me" *(John 14:6)*. There is no access to God the Father or the Holy Spirit without Him. Attending church every Sunday and reading your Bible daily without Jesus won't do it. Following what your pastor says, even doing good deeds alone won't give you access to God. You only get that access to God through Jesus.

This is the truth according to God's Word. Once you settle this part, other parts are simply the icing on the cake. Jesus is the cake. If you'd like a technical example, Jesus is the foundation on which your relationship with God stands. If the foundation is missing, the house won't stand. No one builds a house without laying a foundation. Trying to develop a close relationship with God without Jesus is an exercise in futility.

I am so grateful for what Jesus did to give all humanity access to God. Although, if I am being honest, I wasn't always grateful for what He did and actively ran away from God. It seemed like a boring thing to do, and I didn't want to be boring. I also thought it was something only married women did. I don't even know how I got that mentality, but I did. For many years, if anyone wanted me to follow them for some kind of church event, I would avoid them. I thought they were trying to get me to become boring. In my mind, having a relationship with God and being cool were mutually exclusive. Gosh! I was so wrong.

One day, like Apostle Paul in the Bible, I had an encounter with God. Nothing as dramatic as Paul's but an encounter with Jesus nonetheless. I was away in Kano, in the northern part of Nigeria, doing my National Youth Service. I didn't want to be there as I thought I was missing out on the good life happening in Lagos, where I lived.

On this particular weekend, I had planned to go to Lagos to see my boyfriend at the time. It was his birthday weekend, and the plan was to spend it with him. For some reason that I don't remember now, we argued, and I ended up staying back in Kano. On Sunday, I went to an evening service in the church. As the pastor preached, I felt a prick in my heart that this was what I was meant to do; surrender my life to Jesus. There and then, I did. I have not looked back since. Have I had moments when I wasn't as on fire as I should be? Yes, I have, but I have not given up on my relationship with God. I can tell you for a fact that my life has been far from boring since I gave it to Jesus. It has been full of twists and turns that have surprised even me. Some of my younger family friends even think I am cool. I guess Jesus must be doing something right with me for them to think so.

Before I go on, I want to pause to let you think about your

relationship with God. So let me start by asking the question I got asked that Sunday evening many years ago in Kano, Nigeria. Have you surrendered your life to Jesus and accepted Him as your Lord and Saviour? If you have, I am so glad. It is such an important first step. However, if you have not or have fallen away from Him, can I invite you to say this prayer?

"Heavenly Father, I come to You today through Your Son, Jesus Christ. I have wandered far from Him and done things my way, which before You is sin. I believe in my heart that Jesus is Lord and the Son of God. I believe He died to pay for my sins, and You raised Him from the dead. I confess it with my mouth, and I am saved. Come into my heart today, Jesus, and lead me into a new relationship with God. As I accept You today, I am reborn into the family of God, and I take on His identity. Today is my "birthday." I am born again and now have the Spirit of God in me. In Jesus' name, amen."

Next Step - The Holy Spirit

Well done for taking such a bold step by giving your life to Jesus if you did. Even if you didn't, well done for reading this far and not throwing this book away. If you are still sitting on the fence, why don't you go back a few lines and say the prayer? I promise it is the best decision you will ever make. If you did say the prayer, I am so happy to welcome you into the family of God's cool kids. Not only are you in the family, but you also have the Holy Spirit in you. Do you know how awesome that is? He is the GPS navigation guiding you on your journey. Trust me when I say that He makes all the difference. *(I'll talk more about the GPS navigation system soon).*

As you grow in your relationship with God and yield to the Holy Spirit, your life and journey won't be the same again. I have a name that I like calling the Holy Spirit. I call Him my Director of Affairs. As I have grown in my relationship with God, I have come to realise that I have the Holy Spirit in me. Yet, He is not in me to sit around doing nothing; far from it. That would be like having a useful tool you never use in your house.

Let me be honest: He was not always my Director of Affairs. I don't want you to think I was some saint who got it right from the off. I had been born again for a long time but living a substandard life that no child of God should live. I remember God saying to me some years ago how I could have had a better life as a single woman. Things could have gone a lot better in my earlier years of walking with Him and being single. When I drilled down to why I didn't, I saw there were a variety of reasons. My main ones were not letting the Holy Spirit help me and not using the Word of God as my life's instruction manual.

Even Jesus needed the Holy Spirit when He was on the earth. When He walked the earth many years ago, He did some amazing things with signs and miracles. It was what drew people to Him. People flocked to Him because He had all this power and performed these signs and wonders. All these happened after He was baptised by John the Baptist. The Spirit of God rested on Him and led Him into the wilderness to be tested by the devil.

Jesus could do all He did by the power of the Holy Spirit. When He was born, He came as a man, not as God. When He walked on the earth, He was human like you and me. So, to be able to do any of the things He did, He needed and had the Holy Spirit. When He was leaving, He told His disciples that He was leaving them the Helper, the Holy Spirit. He had already told them they would do even greater works than He did. To do that, He knew they needed the same help that He had. That is why He gave them the Holy Spirit, His Helper *(See John 14:12, 26)*.

Jesus also knew that you and I would need the Holy Spirit to live how God intended. It's why He called Him the Helper in John 14 v 26. I like the Amplified Classic version of that verse. It gives you an insight into the various roles He is willing to play in your life if you let Him. *"But the Comforter **(Counselor, Helper, Intercessor,***

***Advocate, Strengthener, Standby)**, the Holy Spirit, Whom the Father will send in My name [in My place, to represent Me and act on My behalf], He will teach you all things. And He will cause you to recall (will remind you of, bring to your remembrance) everything I have told you."* (emphasis mine).

If you let the Holy Spirit lead you, you will have what I call the Holy Spirit advantage in every life situation. The Holy Spirit will help you in all areas. So much so that you will realise that God is who you have been looking for all along, not a man. He will show you that God fills up a hole in you that can never be filled by a husband, children or even success. It is a lie of the enemy that two halves make a whole marriage. That could not be as far from the truth as possible. The truth is that it is two whole people that make up a good, whole marriage.

That's one of the reasons why you are growing your relationship with God in this season. As you do, He starts to fill that hole in your heart that only God can fill. This is not to say that He will take away your desire for companionship and marriage. Instead, He will bring you to a place where you realise that He is your companion first. He is the only one who can fill that hole. He is the one who meets your deepest needs and desires, not a man. Not only that, His nature is always loving, caring, and thinking about you. Knowing this will ensure that when you finally meet that man, you won't try to make him do what he cannot and should not do.

God does more than fill and satisfy you as you grow your relationship with Him. You will also reap some amazing benefits from being with Him. When you come into a relationship with Him, you gain much more than you bargained for. Here are some of the benefits that I know you will get from this relationship.

Closeness to God

This is what Jesus came for. When man sinned in the garden of

Eden, there was a separation. The man and woman were no longer close to God. There was this space between them. Jesus came to close that gap and restore the relationship so man could be close to God once again. When I surrendered my life to Jesus that day in Kano, I allowed Jesus to close the gap between God and me. There are things I hear and know because of my closeness to God. If I tell you some of the things that happen to me, we'd be here for a while. Sometimes, someone will start sharing something with me, and I'll hear the exact details before they finish speaking. Yes, that's what closeness does for us. Abraham was so close to God that God had to tell him what He was doing before He (God) did it *(see Genesis 18:17)*. Do you know we can get to a place where we know things before others because we are close to God?

Knowing God

With closeness comes knowledge. You can't say you know someone if you aren't close to them. That's how it is between God and us. As I got close to Him, I started to learn His nature and how He spoke and operated. There are some things you cannot convince me otherwise about Him. I have come to know God in such a personal way that I am immovable about certain things. Even tough times can't change my mind about God. So many times, we say we know God, but the truth is that many of us know of God but don't know Him personally. Have you ever heard someone say they know someone famous or popular? Yet, as you start asking questions, you realise they don't actually know the person. That's how it is with a lot of people and God. We know of Him based on what we have heard in church, read on social media, watched on tv or been told by a friend. Only when you start to dig beneath the surface of a person's life, do you realise that they don't know Him that well. It is in this intimate relationship with God that we start to know Him as He is. As we dig into the truth of Him in His Word, the Bible, we begin to know Him and what He wants for us.

Knowing Your Identity

The world is facing an identity crisis. That is the truth. Think about it; isn't the news full of people who are confused about who they are? When I sit and consider what people are struggling with, I see that it comes down to a foundational problem. Most people don't know who they are. It is why they move by the wind of whatever is catchy on that particular day or season. But, after reading this, that will not be you because you will know that God created you in His image and likeness.

You were born female or male as God intended. God wasn't confused when He was creating you. He had an exact image in His mind when He put you together. Not only that, *"But you are a **chosen** generation, a **royal** priesthood, a **holy** nation, His own **special** people, that you may proclaim the praises of Him who called you out of darkness into His marvellous light;"* (1 Peter 2:9). I wish I had a lot more time to explain this point but please, remember those words. Put them somewhere where you can see them often. Say them to yourself daily. You'll see how you begin to flourish even more as you do.

Living a Life of Purpose

If God isn't confused about your identity, then He isn't confused about your purpose. You will discover that you were sent for such a time as this *(see Esther 4:14)*. Being born now in the world, to your family, in your country was not an accident. It was all part of a master plan. God's purpose is on your inside, waiting for you to ask the Purpose Giver to reveal it to you. As you ask, He will reveal it. Not only that, but He will also show you how to fulfil it. That is what we term your calling. The closer I got to God, the clearer I became on what He had called me to do. It was through my relationship and intimacy with Him that I learned more. I got to know who He wanted me to impact with my unique voice and story. Was I confused for a while? Yes, I was. Initially, I thought I was meant to find my purpose when I was meant to seek His purpose for my life. The two aren't the same. One focuses on me as the source of my purpose, while the other focuses on God as the source of my purpose here. I will say that just like your relationship with God is a journey, so is the discovery of your purpose in life. Think of it as many layers that get unravelled as you embark on the journey.

Hearing From God

If there is one question many people ask me, it is, "How do I hear from God?" When they ask, I can see that they are waiting for me to give them a formula. Hearing from God isn't a formula. It is a by-product of being in a relationship. Here's what I mean.

If, for example, your parent or best friend called you and their number came up as unknown on your phone, would you recognise their voice? Your answer is most likely yes. How come you recognised their voice? Is it not because you have a relationship with them and interact with them regularly? The same applies to hearing from God. You recognise Him speaking to you the closer and more intimate you are with Him. That's what a relationship does. The closer you are to someone, the more you come to recognise them. As you grow close to God, you'll become more aware of how He speaks to you. For me, it is via thoughts or impressions in my heart as well as the Bible. Does He use other means? Yes, such as dreams and visions. He will sometimes use other people. He is a multidimensional God, so speaking to us can be done via various means. Grow your relationship with God, and you won't struggle to hear Him speaking to you.

Your Best Life!

Currently, the online world is awash with the phrase "living my best life." When I hear this phrase, I do wonder if they are, or if they are just living someone's definition of what that best life looks like. For me, living my best life is living the abundant life that

Jesus referred to in *John 10:10*. It's living a full, Christ-centred life of abundance and dominion. It is living the life that God had in His heart when He created me. It is not a life devoid of challenges but one where I wake up each day assured that I can overcome those challenges. Jesus said I should relax and be at peace when the challenges come because He has things sorted *(see John 16:33)*. There's so much that I know has come and will still come to me because I am intimate with the Giver of abundance. It is in this knowledge that I choose to rest and live my best life.

There are so many benefits that come from being in a relationship with God. Just thinking about what has happened to me as a person in itself is a benefit. I'll never forget the feeling I had when I read a comment from someone who knew me from my undergraduate days. She posted on my Facebook page about the amazing woman I now was. At that point, I knew I had changed, but for it to be said out loud by someone who knew me before confirmed what I knew to be true. Do you want to be a better version of yourself? Well, a close and intimate relationship with God will sort that out.

Some of the benefits I have listed could be overarching themes with subdivisions. Making the right choice of a life partner, for example, is a side benefit of being led by the Holy Spirit. It could also be a benefit of hearing from God. Good health and healing are benefits of knowing God and the truth of His Word. When you realise what you get with this relationship, it should make you desire to grow it even more. This is the only relationship I know that has limitless benefits. Invest in it.

Reflections

What did I already know that was affirmed in this chapter?

....

What new thing did I learn from this chapter?

....

What can I do with what I now know?

....

What example(s), if any, resonated with me and what didn't?

....

What have I learned that I can start doing right away?

....

Actions

Here are three things I will do based on what I learned in this chapter:

1..

....

2..

....

3..

....

7
Relationship Building Blocks

"Growing your relationship with God is always worth it."
~ *Anon* ~

Having your hunger stirred is the first step in growing your relationship with God. There is nothing wrong with seeking God for the benefits you can get from your relationship with Him. Do not let anyone make you feel bad for seeking Him because of your current needs. God is big enough, loving enough, caring enough to take it. One thing I do know; He will make you desire Him even more as He meets your needs. He can change your heart on the journey.

I started my journey with God because of what I was facing. As the relationship grew, I began to hunger for Him and not only what He could give me. Do I still bring my needs to Him, expecting Him to provide? Certainly. I also desire His presence to know what is on His heart and what He needs me to do for Him. If you've felt bad for coming to God and not being like those you know who seek God for God, don't.

I would encourage you to ask Him to stir your heart for Him. Ask Him to plant a hunger in you, such that all you desire is Him, His presence and doing His will. I can tell you that it is a powerful prayer to pray. Guess what happens as you pray and align your heart with God's like this; all your needs get met. It is a win-win as far as I am concerned.

Having gotten that out of the way, I want to show you how to grow this beautiful relationship with God. What I am about to share isn't a religious checklist of activities that help you grow intimate with God. Remember what I said earlier about this being a relationship, not religion? Keep that in mind as you read the rest of this chapter. Follow the principles and not the example. Too many times, we miss out on our own unique experiences because we copied someone else's example. A path has been tailor-made for you in this relationship with God. Follow it and have the time of your life.

I call what I am about to share the building blocks for growing a relationship with God. Since I am talking about building blocks, let me explain how I look at intimacy with God. I view it as building a house using various materials. The most basic of houses must have a foundation. Then you have the walls that make up the shell before you add the windows, doors and roof. The different activities you do in growing your relationship with God are your building parts. The foundation, walls, doors, windows and roofs all make up your *"Intimacy with God"* house.

What makes your house look the way it does is the design and materials used to build it. The same applies to your relationship with God. Don't look at another's design and wish it was yours. This is a recipe for disappointment. You will think yours is not working or isn't great when it was never meant to look that way. In growing my intimacy with God, I have learned to stop comparing my relationship with anyone else's. It has not been easy, but I have realised that if I am using the basic blocks for building a relationship, I am fine.

How your relationship with God looks will always be different to mine. It is the same as how it would be different to your parents, siblings, friends and even your spouse. Yes, even the way your spouse does their relationship with God will be different to yours. This was one of the things I learned early on in marriage. Talk about a rude awakening. I had thought that my husband and I would be similar when it came to our relationship with God. Well, the first few months started to shake that ideology very quickly. Marriage has been and still is my biggest teacher when it comes to how two people can love God yet have different experiences. So, take the pressure off yourself, focus on your unique journey and enjoy every moment of it.

Now, to the building blocks. What are they?

Praise and Worship

I grew up in an orthodox church. It was an Anglican church with its roots in the Church of England. As such, we sang traditional hymns and chants. Over time, the younger generation in the church got bored with the traditional mode of worship. So they set up a charismatic, Pentecostal-style arm. It was here I first learnt about praise and worship in the way that many know it today. When I moved to the United Kingdom, I started attending a Pentecostal church and the meaning of praise and worship in the way you may know it got cemented.

Praise was the fast-paced song we started the service with, while worship was the slower one we used to wind things down. You may have come to think of those two words the same way I did for many years. That's okay, but I want to tell you that praise and worship are so much more than the songs we sing. When you dig beneath the surface and grasp the full meaning of both words, you will come to realise that they are actions. They are more than music; they are the instructions God commands us to do.

To praise in its simplest form is to boast, commend and joyfully recount. In the blue letter Bible, it even says to be clamorously foolish. Now, that sounds way more than singing a song, doesn't it? When David, a man after God's heart, invites us to praise God in the psalms, he isn't asking us to just sing songs. He says, "Praise!" As Psalm 150:6 points out, if we have breath in our lungs, then we should praise God. It should be our natural response as human beings.

Do you have breath? David says, if you do, you should praise God. He is the One who gave you breath, so why not praise Him? He deserves your praise. Life may be dragging for you right now, and it may seem like your prayers aren't being answered. It could be that life has been tough for you, and you wonder what there is to praise God for. I know those thoughts because I have them too, on occasion. It can seem hard to praise God when things are not going well. Let me share something I learned during one of my low moments.

I had started the year expectant and believed it was the year I would get married. As the year went on, some things happened. I even met someone and, with expectation, started waiting for things to go to the next level between us. Nothing happened. He played this cat and mouse game with me that I now recognise as time-wasting behaviour. Hindsight is such a beautiful thing.

Anyway, I was single, and it was my birthday. I loved celebrating my birthday and Christmas as they were in the same week. But, this birthday was different. I felt my life wasn't where I wanted it to be, and the year was drawing to a close. There didn't seem to be much to celebrate as I didn't have what I wanted. I remember grudgingly going out that evening with one of my friends. While I was out, one of my closest friends called me.

She asked me how my day was going and how I was feeling. I was honest and told her that I didn't feel like celebrating. I was still single when I thought I wouldn't be. Her words to me that day have stayed with me over the years. She reminded me that I was alive, which was enough reason to celebrate and thank God. She spoke other encouraging words that shook me out of my depressing mood. Then she said something that was the icing on the cake. "Bunmi, when you get married, it will happen quickly."

Those were her words to me. At that point, my hope was renewed. I realised that my praise to God could not depend on what had not yet happened. She was right on both points. I had every reason to praise God, and so also do you.

Not having what you are believing for should not stop you from praising God. After that, I kept it in my consciousness as much as possible to praise God even when I didn't feel like it. Praise and worship are not a feeling but an awareness of how good God has been and who He is. If we keep our minds focused on Him, His nature and what He has done so far, we are more likely to praise and worship Him. He is worthy of all that we can give Him and much more. Sometimes, it will be painful to praise Him because things aren't going well or something difficult has happened. I am not saying it will always be easy, but you should still do it. I have praised and worshipped God in some of the most challenging circumstances.

Is it the day my dad passed away or when I got told my chances of conceiving naturally were slim to none? On each occasion, praise got me through. Even as the tears flowed and the pain of loss and disappointment hit me, what came out of my mouth was praise to God. My praise was to the God who sees and knows all things. I sang and praised Him, not because my circumstances were ideal, far from it. I praise God because He deserves my praise, irrespective. Praise moves God. When you praise Him, even in dire situations, you invite Him into that situation. There's something about praising God that moves Him into action. After all, if it weren't so important, it would not be in the Bible.

Praise will cause things to happen for you that you least expect. This is because God inhabits the praises of His people. This means He is present to do what is needed as we praise Him. The Bible is full of so many stories where people praised God, and He went to war on their behalf. I encourage you to try praising Him. It is a weapon that you can use to lift the heaviness that besets single women in their waiting season. As you start to praise Him for what He has done and is yet to do, you will begin to see things happen. Some things will be unplanned but within His plan for you. Praise is a weapon; use it to gain the victory you need.

Worship, on the other hand, is about focusing on who God is. It is an internal connection, a heart position and submission to an awesome God. Worship is a posture of reverence and paying homage to God. Worship has a way of shifting our focus from ourselves and our issues to God and His nature. I love worshipping God, and I can tell you it is more than a song I sing to Him. It is the life that I live. When I live the life that God has called me to and give Him reverence, I am worshipping Him.

Romans 12:1 has made me realise that my life is the sacrifice God desires. My submission to His plan for me is my worship. No one can worship God for me, it is my responsibility, and it should be yours too. Worship has a way of shifting atmospheres because it invites God's heart and presence in. Worship is so God-focused that it causes His presence to sit around us like a blanket. Jesus shows us that worship is a matter of spirit-to-spirit connection, a heart matter. It is not a song we sing *(see John 4:23-24)*.

I look back on my journey and realise that praise and worship got me further than I could ever have gone. On the days when I was low, I would turn on music that lifted praise and worship to God. As I did, the mood would lift. It was undoubtedly a better mood fixer than the supermarket ice cream I loved buying. All that stuff you read in books and watch in movies about the single girl drowning her mood in drink or food is such a lie. They are only temporary, short-lived fixes.

Music can help praise and worship but always remember that they are more than a song.

Prayer

As with my introduction to praise and worship, I was also introduced to prayer as something you do at a set time. I felt guilty all day long when I didn't do it at that set time. Imagine the freedom I felt when I learnt that prayer was communicating with God, a conversation with God. Like me, you may have come to think of prayer in the same way. Something you only do in your quiet time in the morning that is tedious and complicated. It does not help that when we compare ourselves to others, we come up short. By the way, if that is something you do, stop it right now. Jesus and the Word of God are the standards we should seek to meet.

This comparison is why we run away from prayer or think we suck at it. Yet, prayer is one of the key ways we build our relationship with God as it is conversation. Think about your relationship with some of your closest friends or family members. When you are with them, do you compare the relationship with others or simply enjoy their company? Is the conversation filled with big words because you are trying to impress them, or do you just speak? That's how growing a relationship with God, and especially prayer is. No comparison; just free-flowing conversation with each other. Prayer is as simple as saying, "Hi God, I am here again. This morning, my husband said something that upset me. I am struggling to get over it. Can You help me?"

That's how some of my prayers go. The key thing in prayer is communication. In this waiting season, prayer is your opportunity to unburden your heart to God. He knows that you may not like it, but He wants you to say it to Him. Why? Because sometimes, we find the solution we are looking for when we unburden our hearts.

One of the things I have learnt about prayer is that it is a means to partner with God. When I pray, especially when I am praying God's will, I partner with God and bring His will to pass in my life.

I know your next question will be, "how do I know God's will, talk less of praying it?" That one is easy. When you pray the scriptures, you are praying the will of God because they are the will of God. Now, I don't mean the murders, thefts or deception. I mean the scriptures always show us what God desires for humanity, and that includes you. Here's what I do. If I am looking for God's will in a particular area of my life, I search the Bible to find a scripture about it. Then I take the verse, read it, meditate on it, pray and declare it. I have seen so many things happen in my life when I do this.

When I tell people that I have a trick for getting my prayers answered, their eyes light up. I can tell it is because they want the same. The truth is that it is less a trick and more a principle that I have applied from the Bible. If you want answers to your prayers, simply spend time praying with scriptures. As I said, the word of God is the will of God, and God will fulfil His will, not yours. When you pray scriptures, you align with His will and are more likely to get answers. Plus, His will is far better than anything I can ever plan or think for myself *(see Isaiah 55:8-9)*. God says so in those verses in Isaiah 55. Whatever I think is good or even great, He has something better in store. Well, if He does, I want the better of my great. That's why I pray using the scriptures. In doing so, I am ensuring that I am praying for the better of my great.

Let me tell you what happened to me once when I prayed a scripture. I met this lovely guy through a mutual friend, and he seemed like the perfect man for me. He did and said some of the nicest things to me. He even prayed with me during our first conversation, which I found sweet. As the relationship progressed, I started thinking and praying about him more. I asked God to reveal if he was my spouse. I was about to turn thirty and didn't want to waste my time with someone I was not meant to be with. At the time, I went to a women's conference in my church, and the lady speaking said something that struck me. She talked about some of us single ladies being with men and yet not asking God to reveal what the man was like.

She showed us Jeremiah 17:9, *"the heart is deceitful above all things, and desperately wicked; who can know it?"* Then she said we should ask God to show us the man's future file and what he was really like. Guess who did that, thinking she would get a glowing report? Me! Well, I was in for the shock of my life when things turned sour between us, and he said those hurtful words to me.

Now, I am not saying something negative will happen when you pray. No, that's not it. What I am saying is when you pray, especially using scriptures, you are aligning with God's will for your life. Prayer will change the trajectory of your life and take you down God's plan and path for you. Unless you don't want to go down His path, of course. If you do, praying about anything and everything is in your best interest.

Jesus gives us a great model of how to pray in The Lord's Prayer. You can take each line in the prayer and pray it. Each line is both an instruction and an invitation at the same time. Jesus said, *"look, there's a way to pray that covers every aspect of your life. Let me teach you."* I can imagine the atmosphere when Jesus showed his disciples how to pray the right way. It must have changed their prayer lives forever.

One other way I have learned to pray that I want to share with you is praying in the Spirit or praying in tongues. Praying in tongues is letting the Holy Spirit pray God's mind through you. When you do it, not only are you praying with God's mind but also strengthening yourself spiritually. I love praying in tongues as I get to connect with God with no signal interruption. I can't go wrong when I pray in tongues as I am praying in perfect harmony with God's plan for my life. What's there not to love about praying in tongues?

Praying in tongues has become my secret weapon for prayer. I pray in my understanding. But I pray in tongues a lot because it unlocks things in my spirit that I didn't even know were there. I have learned to hone my spiritual senses by praying in tongues. My faith has increased by praying in tongues. If I am feeling a bit flustered about something, I pray in tongues and in time, I become calm and have answers. As I said, it has become my secret weapon.

I have heard people say about prayer, "I don't know if God is near." I can tell you, "He is near." Praying in tongues is a way to keep you aware of Him because it is His Spirit praying through you. Where His Spirit, the Holy Spirit is, there God is. I would love to say more about praying in tongues but let me share a chapter in the Bible you can look up later. It is *1 Corinthians 14*. My goodness, it is such a power-packed chapter on speaking and praying in tongues. Spend some time reading it. Ask the Holy Spirit to help you add praying in tongues to the arsenal in your spiritual toolbox.

Prayer is nothing complicated. Don't let religion make you think that it is or that only some special people know how to pray to get answers. Prayer is talking to God, and it should be a lifestyle. Your life will never be the same when you make it a lifestyle.

Spending Time in The Word of God

I love spending time in the Word of God, but this wasn't always the case. In fact, at one point, I rarely opened my Bible. If you know me, you may struggle to believe that, but it is true. I knew Bible verses, but they were what I had heard in church on Sunday or crammed for a quiz. The challenge with knowing the Word of God this way is that it doesn't get deep down in you. It certainly didn't for me. I knew the verses but didn't know what they meant for me. That's what happens when we know what the Bible says by proxy. When issues come up, we don't know what the Bible says about them or how to apply the Word to them.

It took some challenges for me to start spending time in the word of God. When you run to people who either aren't available or can't give you the answer you are looking for, you can get desperate. That's what happened to me. I was desperate for answers and thought to try the Bible and God. Imagine my surprise when I started getting answers to my challenges. In some cases, the answers came immediately. For others, it took a bit longer.

I have come to look at the Word of God as the instruction manual that we all need. Ever heard the analogy of checking the manufacturer's manual if you want to know how an appliance works? The same applies to us. We are God's creation. To help us function as best as we should, God gave His Word as an instruction manual to guide us in every area of our lives. So, if you are struggling in any area, I highly recommend trying your instruction manual. You may be surprised like I was that the answer you are looking for is in it.

The Word of God is not magic, but it has answers and can transform even the direst of situations. That is why I want to encourage you to spend time in the Word of God daily. It is the food your spirit needs. Just as you eat food daily for your body to grow and be healthy, you also need the Word of God. It is spiritual food for you to grow and be healthy spiritually. You cannot grow as a woman of faith without the Word of God. So even as you read this, I want you to decide to grow by feeding on the Word of God.

As you make that decision, here are some practical tips I would suggest to make it easy. Plan your daily routine with Bible reading and study time into it. It could be in the morning, during your lunch break or before you go to bed. The key thing is to have a consistent time when you do it. Pray and ask the Holy Spirit to help you understand what you are about to read. Start small. Don't set an ambition to read the whole Bible in a year if you don't even read a verse a day. Start with reading a verse, or three, every day. Have a journal to take notes of any thoughts that cross your mind as you read it. Your phone notes can do the same job as the journal. You can even set alarms on your phone to remind you to read a verse or meditate on it. We can't run away from technology, so we might as well use it for good.

I can promise that if you spend time in the Word of God, your life will not be the same again. I was speaking to my best friend one day about how I had become less devil and demon conscious. If you grew up as a Nigerian Christian, then you know what I am talking about. For some reason, as a culture, we seem fixated on demons and enemies in our spiritual walk. This was the background I started my Christian walk in and what I carried going forward. Now, I am not saying that there is anything wrong with being aware of the enemy you are fighting. But you must know when you have exalted that enemy to the same level as God. By the way, they aren't mates. God is the creator, while satan is a creation.

Anyway, I had this conversation with my best friend, and I told her that something had changed in me. I was less devil and demon conscious, and I knew why. Spending time in the Word of God and seeing God daily had shifted my focus. It was not that I had stopped being aware of the enemy and his minions. But by shifting my gaze to God, I had become full of faith. I could see how to deal with any issues that came my way, including dealing with spirits.

The most amazing thing of all is that people started to see that I was a different person. You can have the same too. It just requires you to spend time with God through His Word. There's nothing you are looking for that the Word of God does not have, so go for it. It will be worth it.

Declaring The Word of God

When we pray, we talk to God. When we declare the Word of God, we bring to pass what we want to see in our lives. Think of it like this; one is making a request; the other is establishing what you desire. They are not the same thing, hence why I am sharing with you about making declarations. Job 22 verse 28 tells us that, *"You will also **declare** a thing, and it will be **established** for you"* (emphasis mine). Declarations are a powerful tool that can help change our lives. They are much more than nice, positive affirmations. Using scripture, declarations are power-backed words that go to bat for you.

I love the way my coach describes how declarations work to change your life. When you find scripture and start making declarations, this is what happens. You are introducing new information to your mind. Your mind or heart drives everything about your life. So, if you want to change your life, change the content of your mind. It drives your emotions, thoughts, decisions and actions. This new information then starts to counter the old information in your mind. The new information becomes stronger the more you feed it into your mind, and at some point, your mind starts ignoring the old and starts using the new information.

It is why you may start making declarations about wanting to get married. Then, in time, find yourself attracting men who are husband material. What happened? You started telling your mind that this is the new thing you want. Your mind then starts finding ways to make it happen because that is what you have told it. You may find yourself searching for what you need to do and become to get married. That's your renewed mind finding ways to get you what you have told it you want.

Trust me; I know this one well because it changed how things happened to me when I wanted to get married. As I made declarations about getting married, things started to shift. I started seeing the outward manifestation of what I was saying. Making declarations work across all spheres of your life. I have declarations about every area of my life. When I start something new, I look for scriptures I can declare about it because I know the power of scripture.

In this waiting season, find scriptures about your desire to get married. Look for scriptures about what you desire in your marriage. Some of the ones I used are *Genesis 2:18, Isaiah 34:16* and *Ecclesiastes 4:9-12*. Set aside some time to declare daily what you want to see. Use the verses as your phone screensaver if that will help you remember to make the declaration. In time, your life will catch up with what you are saying.

Fasting

I cannot share about growing your relationship with God without talking about fasting. Yep! Fasting is an important part of the relationship-building process. Doing it helps us draw close to God. I know fasting can be a struggle because I struggled with it for a long time. First, I couldn't understand how to make it through the period of fasting without food. Then there was the struggle not to clock watch till it was time to break the fast. You know what I mean. That constant drifting of your eyes towards the clock to see if it is almost time to eat. But each time you look, you realise it is only five minutes later than the last time you checked.

Don't worry; I am laughing at myself as I write this. You can laugh, too, rather than feel guilty. It happens to the best of us. Yet, Jesus talks about fasting and even says that certain things won't happen without it. I almost want to say in Nigerian lingo, "Oga, how now?" In plain English, how is this possible? Yet, it seems possible because Jesus wouldn't have mentioned it if it wasn't.

If fasting is possible and an important part of growing a personal relationship with God, how do we do it? By the help of the Holy Spirit and with discipline. Self-will only gets you so far, but discipline keeps you going even when you don't feel like it. Add in a good helping from the Holy Spirit, and you will likely find yourself fasting a lot more. That's what I have found. Are there days when I struggle with it? Yes, but I have learned to lean on the Holy Spirit when it comes to fasting. I'd rather try Him than try to do a mind-over-matter stunt.

Fasting does much more when we do it from a Bible-based relationship angle than as a religious exercise. It transforms you as you shed your old self and focus more on the new woman you are becoming. You learn to hear God better as fasting helps with quietening the noise. With fasting, you will learn to prioritise what is important. It will help you focus on what God wants rather than what you want. I feel like God waits for me to start fasting and then uses it to start a heart correction. With fasting, He can recentre you on what is most important, instead of what you desire Him to do for you. This doesn't mean that God won't do what you are fasting about, but something shifts in your heart when you focus on Him. That shift is what the fast is about.

When you read Isaiah 58, you see God's heart about fasting laid out. When I read this scripture in my single days, it started to change how I saw fasting. Even then, I still had all these thoughts about what fasting could do for me rather than what it did in me. In time, it transformed me and my relationship with God. It can do the same for you.

If you have never fasted or aren't used to it, then my encouragement would be to start small. In all things new, start small and grow from there. It's a lesson I have learnt over time that works. Rather than aim for seven days of fasting, why not try even a morning or one day? The whole point isn't the number of days or hours but the connection to God you get as you do so. Whilst you are at it, don't forget to read your Bible. It is your spiritual food. Also, pray and keep the communication lines to heaven open.

When I look back on my journey as a single woman, I am always grateful for the growth of my relationship with God. At the time, I couldn't see the change the way I can now, but the woman I am today was built then. I recently asked God why I am the way I am today. He took my mind back to the many days I spent reading my Bible, journaling and praying for long stretches at a time. I lived alone and didn't have anyone else to cater to but myself, so I spent much of my time with God. I listened to messages by various preachers depending on my need at the time. I searched for answers to questions I had and generally grew as a believer.

When I married and had a child, I didn't have the same luxury of time as I did when I was a single woman. Many times, I had to adjust things to be able to spend time with God in an intentional way. Other times, I was too tired to study my Bible. Having a baby will do that to you. What got me through was what I had built up in my single years.

Don't waste this season. It is a gift that keeps on giving for years to come.

Reflections

What did I already know that was affirmed in this chapter?

....

What new thing did I learn from this chapter?

....

What can I do with what I now know?

....

What example(s), if any, resonated with me and what didn't?

....

What have I learned that I can start doing right away?

....

Actions

Here are three things I will do based on what I learned in this chapter:

1...

....

2...

....

3...

....

"There is no shortcut to a great marriage, and anyone who tells you otherwise is not being kind to you."

8
Detours and Reroutes
(Part I)

"You saw me before I was born. Every day of my life was recorded in your book. Every moment was laid out before a single day had passed."
~ *Psalm 139: 16 NLT* ~

"My parents said you are not my wife."

I was shell-shocked because those were the last words I expected to hear from him. This was the lovely guy that a mutual friend introduced me to and that I prayed about. Things had been going so well between us, albeit faster than what I wanted or was used to. He seemed to tick my boxes, and I was sure that this was heading in the right direction, a marriage that is. I was positive he was genuinely interested in me, and everything he did seemed to point in that direction.

Even the conversation that led to that statement didn't let on that this was coming. It was supposed to be a special day; I was in a good mood, and he was too, but he also seemed off at the same time. It was only after he had dropped this bombshell that it made sense. Nothing like hindsight, right?

All sorts of thoughts started running through my head as I processed what he had said. What did this mean for us? What did he think of what his parents had said? How come they even knew about me? These questions and more flowed through my mind. I tried to come to grips with the reality of the words that had rolled off his tongue.

The first thing I said when I finally found my voice was, *"Okay, how come?"* I wanted to know how his parents were helping him choose me as his wife. He mumbled something about them praying in their prayer group with my name and that of some other lady. At the end of the prayer, the revelation they received was that it wasn't me, and if we went ahead with the relationship, things would end badly between us years down the line.

Wow! As I started processing that part, something struck me. Many things struck me. The one that stood out in capital letters was that there was another woman's name in the mix. Wait, I thought I was the only one he was speaking to, the only one he was trying to get close to? Apparently not.

I felt as though I had been dealt a devastating blow. This was not what I was expecting. He had been so good to me, yet here I was being rejected. Okay, wait. I am running ahead of myself. So, there was another woman significant enough to have her name in the prayer mixer? Who was she? How come he was talking to her at the same time as me?

Now, looking back, I see the feebleness of his explanation. The other woman was a friend. He mentioned her name because they, the praying parents and group, wanted to know all the women in his life. Why mention her name if she was only a friend? That's what came to my head, but I had fallen for this guy, and sadly, I accepted his explanation at the time. Let me be honest and say that I accepted it, but I didn't. A part of me closed off even though I accepted it.

"Where do we go from here?" was the question on my mind. We had all these plans, but forget the plans; I wanted to know what

he thought of what his parents had said. He said it was confusing for him as he liked me a lot but knew his parents also wanted the best for him. I could understand that, but at the same time, I felt he should be a man about it.

I was navigating this without my parents. First, I was of the age of consent and second, I wanted to have a conviction that was mine. So, I asked him what God was saying to him. He didn't know what God was saying, but he still wanted us to see each other whenever he visited. He lived in another country at the time.

The day after he dropped the bombshell, my lovely dad died. Talk about heartbreak upon heartbreak. The funny thing was he, the guy, still called me that morning to pray with me. It was something we had done since we met. Even though we had this cloud hanging over us, we still did it, prayed together, that is. It was shortly after getting off the phone with him that I got the call about my dad's passing. And guess what? He was the first person I called. That's how close we were.

He came to visit me, and we had an amazing time, but I kept having this feeling of all not being well. I guess being told I was not his wife and still trying to push through would do that to one's psyche. Eventually, I couldn't take it anymore and asked him what was happening. He felt we should take a break so he could seek clarity from God on our relationship. *"Oh, so even though I had asked, you hadn't thought to do that?"*

What I thought would be a quick break to give him the much-needed slap on the head turned into weeks and months. In time, I had to accept that we were not meant to be. It hurt a lot. I felt rejected. My hopes of a great relationship were dashed once again. Disappointment swept over me, but I also had the grief from losing my dad holding me in its grip. It was a double whammy for me at that time.

Looking back, I realise it was a time that shifted the trajectory of my life. As I reflected more about life and losing my dad, I started coming to a new understanding of many things. The reality of life is that we will not be immune to challenges. Some of them will come to us of their own making, whilst others we may willingly draw into our lives. I call these our detours. They are circumstances and situations that happen and seem to set us off the course we want or are supposed to be on. Sometimes, we create these detours through our choices or actions we take or don't take. Other times, life will throw us these detours, like in the case of my dad dying. It is up to us to decide how we get back on track.

As with all detours, if we want to get back on track, we will have to reroute ourselves. It is like the GPS navigation system we are so used to these days. We put in our destination, Google maps shows us the route, and we start moving. Of course, if we don't move, the map doesn't work, but that is not the crux of what I am saying now. That is by the side. You know what, let me pause and say something here.

You may be at a point in your life where you want to move forward as you sense there is more for you. That's a good thing. But, if you don't move, you won't get to where you sense you should be. What does it mean to move? It means to reflect, plot your route, and then act. So, don't stay stuck in analysis paralysis and not move at all. Are you scared to try? At least dip your toe in the water and see if it gets bitten by a crab or if the water is too cold. You won't know without trying.

Now, let's get back to Google maps, routes and getting to destinations. Most people tend to use Google Maps to plot their route to a destination. If you are familiar with Google maps, you know that most times, it plots multiple routes to a destination and, depending on your settings, it tends to put the fastest route at the top of the list. Then, all things being equal, if you follow that route, you will get to your destination at the estimated time.

Now, if you are unfamiliar with the route or haven't learned to use Google maps well, you may take a wrong turn. That's called a detour.

What Google Maps does for you to get you back on track is recalculate the route. It will find the nearest turning that will bring you back on the route to your destination. You may have to take a few extra streets to get back to the main road. Or it may find an alternative main road close to where you are at the time that can get you to your destination. This means taking an alternative, but still the quickest, route to get you to your destination. If you stick with that route, you'll reach your destination but maybe a little later than planned. What helps Google keep on track with the plotted route is the GPS tracker. The GPS tracker scans the area, pulls up the streets on the map and helps plot the best route to take if you've detoured off the planned one.

I now want you to think of our subject matter in this book, *marriage*. That is our destination. To get there, God has a route for us, which depends on the marriage we are meant to have. As we start proceeding through life, we will take turns. Depending on your relationship with God and understanding of His plans, you may submit to His route. In doing that, you end up at the destination at the estimated time. This does happen. Some people meet God early on in life and start following His plan for their lives. As such, they end up where He wants them to be when He wants them to be there.

Others like me, and maybe you, don't always stick to the planned route. We take a wrong turn, or two, or five and need to get back on track. Who helps to put us back on track? The Holy Spirit! Like the GPS tracker, He can scan where we are and see the best route to put us back on track. He is one of the best gifts given to us by God after Jesus. It's why Jesus said in *John 14: 16* and *16:13* that He would give us a Helper who would guide us. We were never meant to do the journey of life alone. In His wisdom, God gave us an internal GPS tracker, the Holy Spirit, to keep us on track.

When we take these detours, it's usually because we aren't following the route, have missed our turning or are unfamiliar with how the tracker works. This is why I shared about your relationship with God and His Holy Spirit earlier on.

Now, let us spend some time looking at the detours that happen on this journey to marriage. Detours can happen but remember this. With every detour, there is a recalculated route available.

As I experienced a detour with the guy I spoke about earlier, you also may have experienced a detour too. The joy and hope I want to offer you now are that when we experience these detours, there are alternative routes. If we follow these routes, we will eventually reach our destination. But we must follow the route and aim to stay on course.

Some detours are likely to happen on the journey to marriage. As we go on, I will share what they are and how you can find alternative routes. So, stick with me; if you've gone off track, we'll get you back on course. You can and will get back on track.

Detour One – Heartbreak

Was I heartbroken after the experience I talked about earlier? Most definitely. Not only was my heart broken, but some things happened when he came back on the scene that hurt. Oh, yes, he came back after about ten months, but things didn't go much further as we had a bad falling out. Many years later, he sent me a message to apologise for how things ended.

When we had the falling out, he said some hurtful things, and I was so upset. Not only was I hurt, but I was also heartbroken. Even though it had taken ten months to reconnect, the feelings I had before came back to life. The night we had this falling out,

I remember going to bed upset and annoyed as I didn't think I deserved what he said to me. The following day, I woke up and wanted to pray. As I started, the Holy Spirit told me to stop. He said He wanted me to pray for him.

"You must be joking, right? He was the one who hurt me!" I didn't see why I should be the one praying for him, but the Holy Spirit didn't budge. I had to pray for him. Grudgingly, I opened my mouth and started praying. The tears started flowing as I couldn't hold back the pain. I wept as I prayed and blessed him with prayers and declarations that I would have made over myself. At that moment, it was painful, but I did it. When I finished, I sensed heaven smile on me and said, *"Now you can pray."* After that kind of experience, my prayer was simple, *"Don't let him meet me single when he comes back."* He didn't.

That was the beginning of my healing journey. If or when you experience heartbreak, you must heal. It is important for you as a person. A fragmented heart attracts fragmented experiences and people. Untreated heartbreak is like an untreated wound. It will fester and, in time, wreak more havoc than when it was a fresh wound. That's why you must treat it.

Getting into another relationship to mask or dull the pain is not the solution. That is a recipe for disaster. If you go into a relationship straight after a heartbreak, you are likely to use that person. You will try to use them to fix what went wrong. The relationship becomes a plaster over a wound that needs surgery. Isn't that too much pressure to put on another person? Your heart needs time to heal, and that can only happen by taking a break from all heart entanglements. You deserve a whole love, but your heart can't recognise and accept that kind of love if it is hurting.

God knows this, hence why He made me pray for the guy. It wasn't the only thing that I needed to do for me to heal, but it was the starting point. So often, we try to use external things to deal with something that needs internal work. Don't get me wrong. The external things we do to heal are good, but they can never replace the internal work that needs to happen. When we only do external things, we are doing what I said earlier; putting a plaster over something that requires surgery.

I will touch on some of the external things but let's start with the internal ones. Being a woman of faith, I would do you a disservice if I didn't tell you to start with prayer. Pray about the relationship and how things ended. Pour out your heart in prayer because I can tell you that it is the one place where you can be completely vulnerable. Before you unburden to your best friend or even a therapist, pour it out to the One who loves you and wants to help you heal. He is deeply interested in your healing, and His heart hurts for you. Tell Him how you are feeling. Don't hide anything. This is a part of the process that you need more than you may realise. You are talking to a Person, not some abstract God who sits afar off and has no interest in your life. He is right beside you and wants you to tell Him where it hurts.

I have come to realise that prayer during heartbreak prevents bitterness. Praying releases the ill-feeling you may have towards the other person. As you do so, you may realise that you don't need to unburden to someone else. I am not saying you can't, but you may not need it. Also, if you are going to unburden yourself to anyone about how you are feeling, you want two things in that person. One, a safe, judgement-free, empathetic place. Two, a place where you can find help on your journey. If your unburdening will only rehash what happened, then the conversation is unnecessary.

Talking to a trusted friend, a counsellor, or even a relationship coach is one of the external things we can do. The purpose of these conversations is to help you navigate the healing journey. If you go to a counsellor or coach, you will likely move along the healing journey faster. They have the training and experience to help you navigate this phase. They will have the extra tools and resources you need to get over the heartbreak. They tend to know more than you about how to get you back on your feet. Does this mean you can't navigate this experience by yourself? Sure, you can, but why take twice as long when God has put around you what you need to get back on route quicker?

What other things could you do to overcome heartbreak? Take time to review what happened. This is not in a bid to make you sad or more depressed but to help you understand what happened. Ask yourself some vital questions such as, "What happened?" "What part did I play in this?" "What did I notice about myself and the other person?" "What learnings can I draw from this experience?" This is where you put on your big girl pants, take responsibility and do the hard but needed work for your healing.

Be honest with yourself as you answer these questions. Don't shy away from the uncomfortable truths you may encounter. I want you to acknowledge the truths you learned about yourself and the part you played. I can tell you that it is better to know those truths now and change if needed than to continue in ignorance. Ignorance isn't bliss. Ignorance will keep you on detours and prolong the journey to your destination.

For you to heal, I would also recommend you reduce or stop contact with the person who broke your heart. I know you may still have feelings for him, but keeping the lines of communication open won't help. Doing so whilst trying to heal is like opening the wound again and again. You know how we women do. Even though we are heartbroken, we still hold out this modicum of hope that maybe things will work out. We hope that we will get back together. So, we reach out to him, or we still keep responding when he calls. Darling, it won't help! Even if you get back together, and I am not saying you will, you still need to heal. Something caused the initial heartbreak, and it needs to be treated. Broken bones need to be reset, and they need to heal before they can be used again. So, also, do you.

On your journey of healing, find a support system that you can lean on. Before you say I don't have that, I want you to think about the relationships in your life. Are you saying there is no one you can turn to and ask for help? They may not be your likely choice but could be the needed one. When I was getting married, my husband and I talked about getting marriage mentors. We knew that we needed the support. As we scanned the couples we knew, we listed three couples we thought would be ideal.

I had a particular couple who I thought was perfect, but God chose the couple I least expected. They have been amazing to us. My point is this; there are people in your life who you may not yet recognise as your ideal support system. If you open your eyes and heart, you will see them. If you still think you do not have anyone, I want to challenge you to become that support system for someone else. You'll be amazed at how you will attract a support system of your own. It's called the principle of sowing and reaping.

This *heartbreak* detour is a painful one and one you might experience on the journey to marriage. That's life. The key is to take the necessary steps to reroute yourself back on track when it happens.

Detour Two – Disappointment

Not far behind heartbreak is the disappointment detour. This one often paints a picture of lost hope. Another relationship had gone down the drain. That relationship you were so sure would end in marriage is now over. Disappointment brings a wave of hopelessness with it. When you meet someone or start a relationship, you have hopes and expectations. I know I did with my previous relationships. In some cases, I built up my expectations so high that I would be floating on the clouds. Imagine crashing down from the clouds. It is painful.

On the journey to marriage, I detoured a lot with disappointment. I kept building up expectations in relationships that, in hindsight, I shouldn't have. As an unmarried woman, I wore my heart on my sleeve a lot. This opened me up to disappointment when my affections weren't returned. I wanted to be in a relationship so much that I was willing to give my heart, and in some cases my body, away. All he had to do was show interest in me.

I now know that this was a recipe for disaster. I should never have given my affections away like that. They were precious, and only a worthy person deserved them. I remember one guy; let's call him Mike. I met him at a wedding, and we seemed to hit it off. He did the right things and said the right words, so I gave him my number. I then proceeded to sit by the phone, waiting for him to call, which he did in the end. We then started this cat and mouse game, flirting on the phone but never going any further. I would give off signals showing him I was interested, but he never seemed to catch on. Or maybe, he was pretending not to so as not to commit.

You may be wondering why I was disappointed. After all, it was clear that he was not interested in taking the relationship any further. Well, at the time, it wasn't that clear to me because he kept giving me mixed signals. He had a way of making me feel special, and this made me think a relationship was on the cards. That's why I built up my expectations. Plus, he had all the makings of a good husband, which made me hang on that little bit longer.

I should have moved on from the friendship, but I held on for a little while longer. I am almost sad to say that I held on for years, hoping against hope that things would go further. Whenever I thought, *"there's nothing here for me,"* he would call and start the flirtation all over again. With time, I got the point and stopped hoping. Once again, I had been hit with disappointment. Things hadn't panned out; I was still single!

Looking back, I wonder why I allowed myself to get into these scenarios. This wasn't the first time I was disappointed and had my hopes dashed. It wasn't even the second time. Remember I said I wore my heart on my sleeve and was quick to give my affections away? Looking back, here's what I learned. With each one, I realised it was because I had opened myself up too quickly. I began planning a life with someone who wasn't thinking on the same wavelength as me.

You might be like me or not. Disappointment is something you will likely encounter on your journey to marriage. I did. I have a prayer journal filled with hopes and dreams of relationships that never were. Don't let me get started on the prayers I prayed based on my hopes and expectations. If I could have twisted God's arm to make my hopes come to pass, I would have. I begged and pleaded with God. I declared scriptures and prayers about relationships. I even sowed financial seeds in one relationship, hoping it would end in marriage. That didn't happen.

Are there ways to protect yourself from disappointment? Yes, there are but let me first deal with how you overcome it if or when it comes knocking on your door. As with heartbreak, you should start with prayer. By now, I'm sure you have realised that I am a big fan of praying about everything, and I mean everything. Prayer is a key tool you need in your bag of life toolkit. Use it always. Pray about your disappointment. God wants you to pray about it and hand it over to Him. He says so in *Psalm 55:22*. He promises that as you do so, He will take care of you. Can you imagine that? He isn't judging you for opening yourself to disappointment.

He is thinking of how to help you so you can get back on route to where you desire to be. So, run into His open arms through prayer. Lay it all down with Him. Cry if you must. Do what you need to do as He leads you on a journey back to wholeness. Maybe you don't want to pray to Him because He has upset you. You feel that He, God, that is, let you down by allowing the disappointment to happen in the first place. Let's talk about that for a minute or two. Don't worry; I am not going to ask you to say it out loud but can you be honest with yourself? Are you mad at God for what has happened to you? Why are you angry with Him? Can you process that? It's okay; I'll wait.

Are you done? Were you able to answer those questions? We often get angry with God for our unmet expectations because we believe He should meet them. This is especially true if you are a believer praying to Him about the relationship. Now, I am going to say something you may not like, but I want to help you here. I would rather present you with the truth than let you continue being angry with Him. God isn't obligated to meet our expectations if they don't align with His will for our lives. Do you need to read that again?

This leads to the next thing I want you to process. Were your expectations in line with God's will for your life? Was He the leading force behind those expectations? Or were you in the driving seat asking Him to validate your desires and hopes? I know you may feel like flinging this book out of the window at this point but hold on. I know I am asking some uncomfortable questions, but I want you to know that this is for your good. Please keep going.

So, was God at fault? Were there red flags you ignored? Did you pay attention to the clues He may have raised in you about your relationships? Can you see where this line of questioning is heading? It's not that I want to make you feel bad, but I want you to take time and reflect. Is your upset with God misplaced? Could it be that you were partly to blame for what happened? The truth is God loves you and wants the best for you. Yes, you've heard that before but do you believe it? If you do, you are less likely to be mad at Him for the disappointment you face. Believe and accept His love for you. He isn't happy when you deal with disappointment. It was never in His plan for you, and He wants to help you overcome it.

Even as you begin to accept His love, I want you to spend some time reflecting on how you got here. The questions I asked are a good starting point as you need to reflect on what has happened. As you start looking to the future, I want you to reflect on the source of your expectations. Where did they come from? Your background? What you've read in a book *(hello, Mills & Boon)*? Was it how your family and friends were in their relationships? You'll be amazed at the things that create our expectations. I can't even begin to tell you some of my expectations of men and relationships. A funny one was expecting my now husband to bring flowers on our first date. You may say there's nothing wrong with that. True, there isn't, but imagine if I had based my decision on if he was a good catch by him bringing flowers or not. People have made choices using flimsier standards. So, what are the sources of your expectations? Are they wholesome expectations or what others sold to you?

The next step is to consider how you will manage your expectations in the future. Pacing your expectations when you meet someone new is a good place to start. Take things slowly, and don't rush. Before you jump into planning your future together, consider the relationship level. Is this person an acquaintance, friend or someone deeper? When you're clear on a person's place, it becomes easier to manage your relationship expectations. There are certain expectations you have of your friends that you don't have of an acquaintance. This is because you know the depth level of the relationship.

Even if the guy is keen to rush things along, take time to get to know him as a person. Build a friendship that is devoid of exclusivity. So many of our disappointments are because we make relationships exclusive very early. We don't get to know the person before we give them the title of boyfriend. I know that society's way of doing things is to get into the relationship first before finding out about them. I can tell you that this causes many a broken heart and failed expectations. You can be friends with a guy without being in a relationship with him. Take the pressure off the relationship and just be friends. Disappointment is less likely to come knocking on your door that way.

Reflections

What did I already know that was affirmed in this chapter?
....

What new thing did I learn from this chapter?
....

What can I do with what I now know?
....

What example(s), if any, resonated with me and what didn't?
....

What have I learned that I can start doing right away?
....

Actions

Here are three things I will do based on what I learned in this chapter:

1. ....
....
2. ....
....
3. ....
....

9

Detours and Reroutes
(Part II)

"See any detour as an opportunity to experience new things."
~ *H. Jackson Brown Jr.* ~

I not only experienced heartbreak and disappointment on my journey to marriage. Oh, if only those were the only detours I experienced, but sadly there were more. You may have experienced some of the ones I am about to share. If you have, I pray you will find the answers you need to get back on course if you haven't already.

Detour Three – Rejection

Apart from dealing with heartbreak and disappointment, I also tangled with rejection. This particular detour messes with your mind big time. This detour can be a bummer if you haven't spent time building yourself up and having a healthy view of who you are. It can keep you off track for a while. With each failed relationship, you may feel like you are being dealt a bad hand time and time again.

There is something that rejection does to your psyche. It takes you down a rabbit hole and sells you the lie that you are not good enough. That's the biggest message of rejection. It attacks your self-worth and paints a picture where you come up short. If you stay with that message, it will seep into your heart which is the seat of beliefs. Beliefs determine what happens to us. When you believe you aren't good enough, you can become a magnet that attracts men who affirm that belief. It is a vicious cycle and a rabbit hole you don't want to go down or stay in.

I know this all too well. It started when I was in my teens. I felt rejected by boys because I wasn't *pretty* enough. Now, don't ask me why I was thinking about boys in my teens. I blame my raging teenage hormones and the sappy romance novels I was reading at the time. You don't realise what seeds are planted in your mind by words and actions until they start bearing fruits. I got told by people that my sister was prettier than me. If we happened to be together, she often got more attention than me. University years were no different. It didn't help that I wore glasses and teeth braces. All this led to some stinking thinking and beliefs about myself. As the years passed and I waited for marriage, each rejection reinforced that belief.

I was saved from this warped thinking through an audio message I heard by the late Pastor Bimbo Odukoya. She was a pastor and thought leader in the relationship industry many years ago. I can't even remember the title of her message, but I remember what she said. Her words put my feelings of rejection to bed once and for all. She said something along these lines, *"Single sister, it seems like no one is interested in you. God is hiding you because you are precious and special."* I had never considered that rejection was a blessing in disguise. When you want something so bad, anything that stops it seems like a curse, but that phrase was a deliverance for me. It put me on a path to wholesome thinking about myself and helped me overcome my pain and hurt. I realised I was special, and if any man I met didn't see that, it was his loss. That phrase by Pastor Bimbo would ring true much later when men weren't paying me any attention. Boy, that was an interesting phase in my journey.

Crickets were what I would use to describe that phase. You know when it is quiet, and all you hear is the sound of crickets? That's how it was. When people asked me who was on the scene, my response was, "no one." They often thought I was telling tales, but it was the truth. It seemed as though there was this veil over me. Even though I was meeting men, nothing ever went past the first introduction. It was that phrase from Pastor Bimbo's message that helped keep my self-esteem intact. Imagine if I didn't understand that I was precious to God and that He was protecting me? I would have spiralled into depression based on thinking I wasn't valuable enough.

As I reflect now, I realise that God was kind to me even though I didn't feel He was. He drew me in when I was low. There were times I would ignore the invitation and try to run away from Him, but He was persistent. His love for me was unchanging. Whenever I faced rejection, He came alongside me and reminded me that I was extra special to Him. You are special to God. Even though it feels like no one else appreciates that, I encourage you to keep that truth in your heart. Never doubt it.

Rejection has a way of making you feel like you have no worth. It tells you that you aren't pretty enough and that you need to do something to make yourself more attractive. It will sell you lies about who you are, and if you entertain them, you will eventually buy into that faulty thinking. Yes, we are all a work in progress, but we can be a masterpiece even on the journey to where God is taking us. Fighting the lies that come with rejection was the biggest mental battle I had to overcome. Gradually I came to realise that I was fearfully and wonderfully made, with no mistake in who God made me *(see Psalm 139:14)*. My soul needed to know this. It was the only way I could handle the rejection.

Over time, I became more familiar with knowing that I was special to God and that He didn't make a mistake when He made me. I also spent time learning about my worth in Him. It is this understanding that keeps you grounded when rejection comes knocking. You must spend time delving into your identity and worth as an individual. Knowing the truth of God's word about your identity is the first step to dealing with rejection. It's not only something to pray about; you must also have a belief system about yourself grounded in the unshakeable word of God. It was only when I understood that I was special to God that the feelings of rejection started to fade away. Here are a few things that God thinks about you that you may not know.

You are special, so special that He sent Jesus to die for you. Every time He sees you, He sees something good. God didn't make a mistake when He made you. You are His child, and He would do anything for you. Even when you mess up, He still loves you and will always love you. His thoughts towards you are always good and loving. You are beautiful. When He was fashioning you in your mother's womb, He was painting a masterpiece. You are stunning in His sight.

You can personalise these words, by the way. You must accept who you are to overcome rejection. You must also acknowledge that you were rejected. This is one thing you may not want to do because it is painful, but it is also freeing. It puts the ownership of the rejection on the person who rejected you as it was their choice, not yours. I know this goes without saying, but I will say it so you can get off this detour. Don't stay in a place where you are continually rejected. I said some moments ago that you are special. Anyone who doesn't appreciate how special you are does not deserve you. I'll say it again. Anyone who doesn't appreciate how special you are does not deserve you. Does this mean that you don't need to improve yourself? I am not saying that, but I want you to remember that there is nothing wrong with being a masterpiece and a work in progress at the same time. Doing this will help you move on instead of trying to hold on to someone who doesn't want to be with you. This is how you get back on the route to your destination.

As I have already mentioned, spend time praying. Pray for yourself, for a full revelation of who you are and how valuable you are. It is a reality that you need to build into your psyche. Also, tell God how you feel. There's nothing wrong with saying, *"I am so sad right now"*, *"I thought he was the one"*, or *"I feel so rejected."* You can bawl your eyes out. There is nothing you bring before Him that He hasn't heard or seen before. Be honest with Him. But please, pray.

Pray for strength, healing, and wisdom. You need strength to get back up again. Healing is important so that you aren't bitter from the experience. Unforgiveness towards the person who hurt you will only keep you stuck in the same place. You must move on because your future depends on it. Don't let unforgiveness hold you back from a great guy who thinks you are amazing and wants to shower you with love. When you pray for wisdom, it is so that you can manage your interaction with the person going forward. In my case, it was wise to stop communicating with any of those guys. I knew I still had feelings and interacting with them even as "friends" was not going to do me any favours.

In some cases, I blocked the guy's number so he couldn't call me. I wasn't taking chances with my heart anymore. You shouldn't either. Do what you need to do to move forward and get back on track. The feelings of rejection don't last forever *(see Psalm 30:5)*, but you must desire to move on. You can stage a comeback from rejection, get back on track and arrive at your destination. When you look back, it will be like a hazy dream that you vaguely remember, that is, if you even remember at all.

Detour Four – Doubts and Complaints

You know I had to go there, didn't you? You didn't? Well, this is a major detour, and I know that if I don't talk about it, I will be doing you a disservice. Don't worry, I am not judging you for this particular detour as I am a recovering doubter and complainer myself. I have gotten better with time, and I am thankful for that. In hindsight, I realise how much these two siblings *(yes, they are siblings)* took me off track.

Before you say, "I am not doubting God or complaining about this season," let me break down what they are. When I am done, if you are still convinced, then you can move on to the next detour. But, if a little niggle tells you there are some traces of these siblings in you, please take time to deal with them. I want you back on track as soon as possible. There's no need to stay on this particular detour because they take you nowhere fast. You don't want that. I don't want that for you either. You deserve the marriage you desire, and you must not let doubt and complaints stop you from getting it.

I remember a point in my waiting season when I doubted if marriage would happen for me. If you had asked me if I doubted, the answer would have been no. Who wants to admit something like that? I didn't. It would have spoilt my "Christianese" façade, and I wasn't having that. Yet, in my heart of hearts, I was scared. The years were passing by, and it wasn't happening for me. The more I met men and things didn't pan out, the more I wondered if I would get married. This led to complaints as I compared myself to those getting married. *"How come she's getting married, and I am not?" "What does she even know about marriage?" "Why did You (God) bring me down this path?" "What am I doing wrong?"* I never muttered the complaints out loud. As I said, I couldn't let anyone think I wasn't standing in faith for my marriage. Yet, they were there.

Then came the turning point. I call it a turning point because something switched on in me as soon as it happened. I realise now that I had an encounter that birthed conviction. Conviction is important because it is the lack of it that we call doubt. When we lack conviction, we start to complain because we are not satisfied with the outcome of our desires. Yet, the thing is, your desire won't change until you change your conviction. See why I said doubt and complaints are siblings. One gives birth to the other.

I started building my conviction about marriage, and at this point, I must say it was the Word of God that helped me. Romans 10:17

says, *"So then faith comes by hearing, and hearing by the word of God."* I spent hours in the Word searching for scriptures where God had spoken about marriage. As I found them, I would feast on them, pray with them, and make declarations about my marriage using them. Conviction or faith isn't accidental. It must be built up, and no one can give it to you. It is something you must actively reach for yourself.

This is the time to counter your doubts with faith that your desire for marriage will happen. Search the scriptures. Find what it says about marriage. One scripture I believed beyond a shadow of a doubt was Isaiah 34:16. I was sure I would not want for my spouse. The Holy Spirit would bring us together, giving us eyes to see and recognise each other at the right time. It happened as I believed.

Doing this built up my conviction that I would get married. My final turning point came one cold February evening in church. The singles ministry had planned a week of prayers for our marriages; this was the last night. I didn't live near the church at the time, so I had to drive about an hour and a half to get there. Being a Friday night, I could finally be present in the chapel to join the prayers in person rather than online. I remember that encounter as though it only happened yesterday.

Before this day, I had been asking God why I was still single. I wanted to be sure that if I was doing something wrong or had an area of my life to work on, I was doing it. Each time I asked, I got radio silence. He spoke to me about other things but didn't answer this particular question. It didn't mean He didn't hear, but in His wisdom, He knew I wasn't ready for the answer. So, imagine being in this prayer meeting and hearing this question: **"Do you know why you are still single?"** I immediately stopped praying. I knew it was God speaking. Hearing God was something I had been growing in, so I knew He was the one speaking to me.

This was the moment I had been waiting for. I think I muttered something like, "No, but I guess You are about to tell me." He then asked me a strange question. I found it strange because of the words He used. He showed me a family member and asked, "What is she?" I was confused because I didn't understand what He meant. Then He said another family member's name and asked the same question using the word "what." This is why I love God. As He spoke, I immediately saw a pattern between both of them, and it was as though a light had switched on in my mind. I got it! It was a pattern that was common not only to them but also to other family members. I had never seen it before that conversation. As what He said dawned on me, He proceeded to tell me that it would not happen with me and that I would get married.

The basis for why I would get married was who I was in Christ. Although there was a negative pattern in my family, it no longer applied to me. As a born-again Christian, a believer in Christ, I was free from negative patterns. Christ's death and resurrection on the cross had set me free. I was no longer subject to that pattern. This is true for you, too, if you are a believer. Christ has given you a brand-new identity that doesn't come with negative patterns. Even if you are still experiencing those patterns as a believer, I am here to tell you that you can be free. Knowing who you are in Christ and what He did for you will help you change things. If you are not a believer, that's okay. You've had the opportunity to give your life to Christ in this book. I hope you took it.. I am a witness of Jesus Christ, and as much as it is within my power, I will introduce Him to you. By the way, you aren't compelled to give your life to Him, but I pray that as you see what He did for me, you will desire Him too.

God's words to me on that cold Friday evening in the chapel were a major source of peace. His words birthed a conviction in my heart. I became resolute that no matter how long it took, I was going to get married. After that encounter, there was no situation before me that could change my mind. I no longer doubted that it would happen. I also stopped complaining. That encounter birthed conviction in me. By the way, encounters aren't only angelic visitations and trances. A simple word from God, like mine, can be an encounter that changes the trajectory of your life forever. That's what encounters do; they birth conviction and build your faith. In doing so, they help you be all that God wants you to be on this side of eternity.

For many years, I was no different to the Israelites who complained after they left Egypt. All through their journey to the promised land, it was one complaint or the other. Although they were recipients of God's goodness, favour, mercy, kindness and power, they often forgot what He had done for them. You might say, "Well, I am not like them," but are you sure you're not? How quickly have you forgotten what God has done and is currently doing in your life? What happened to the miracles, signs, and wonders that you have been a recipient of? It is human nature to forget, so don't feel too bad. Forgetting doesn't make you a bad person. It is why the patriarchs of old had landmarks to remind them of where they had encountered God. This was a wise move that you and I should copy.

Landmark reminders produce gratitude which is the antidote to complaining. Gratitude must become a conscious action for you in this season. Take time to write down what you are grateful for each day. Spend a few minutes saying thank you to God for where you are right now. Remember, you can thank Him at any time and any place. Find ways to incorporate it into your daily routine. Is it for just being able to breathe? That's one thing you should be thankful for daily. Does your body function the way it should? Are you able to eat? Do you have the means to get to school or work? Are you surrounded by friends and family? Is there one meal left in your fridge? You ought to thank Him!

Trust me, there is so much to be grateful for if you take the time to reflect on your life. Don't lose out on the beauty and blessings of this season because you are so focused on what is not yet here. Only two people in a whole generation of people amongst the children of Israel made it to the promised land. The rest died because of their complaints and doubts. That is a sobering thought, but it also shows you what can happen when you stay in a place of doubt and complaints. This won't be you because you will change from today. You will get back on route to your promised land.

Detour Five – Sex and Past Sins
I wasn't a virgin when I got married. From an early age, I meddled with sex. When I look back on my life, I am grateful to God. Do you know what I am grateful for? That He saved me from sins that could keep me completely off track. When I look at my husband and marriage today, all the glory belongs to God. He doesn't leave us in our sin but draws us to Himself. That's what He did for me, and I know He can and will do the same for you if you accept His invitation. I know staying pure is hard. We live in a society and culture that is highly sexualised. You get told that everyone is doing it, including those in church, so why shouldn't you? I have heard tales of families that won't let their children marry unless they test the goods first. They say it is to ensure that all is working as it should. That may be a rule that applies to your family. Whichever way you turn, sex is right in your face. You don't have to go far to see it; be it the adverts on tv, general conversations or content on social media.

It's no wonder we succumb to it. I know I did. Not only did I succumb, but I stayed in it for a long time. Even when I gave my life to Christ, it was an area that I struggled with. I knew I wasn't meant to do it, but that didn't stop the urges. Becoming a believer didn't automatically change my mindset about sex or that men needed sex to stay with me. Don't let anyone tell you the lie that everything changes the second you give your life to Christ. That's not true. Your spirit man becomes brand new *(2 Corinthians 5:17)*, but your mind still needs renewing. It has fed on a lot of junk over the years, and those things don't just disappear overnight. That's why we still struggle with sex and sin after we become born again. It is also why Apostle Paul encourages us to renew our minds *(Romans 12:2)*. He knew that receiving Jesus into your heart and life wasn't enough. You had to be intentional to change what was in your mind. As you do so, your desires and appetites will change. It is a journey, not an instant one-time event. As you renew your mind daily in the Word of God about your identity and purpose, you will start to see a change. That is what happened to me, but first, I had to understand what sex was. I also had to know the impact it has when you have it within the confines of marriage.

Sex is a beautiful gift from God to mankind, but He always intended it to be within the confines of marriage. It was never meant to happen whilst we were single or unmarried. Genesis 2: 24 tells us that the man and woman will become one flesh, something which occurs when we have sex. Going by where this verse is in the Bible (before the enemy showed up), it's easy to see that sex was all part of God's original design. Sex is good, holy and a gift from God. The fact that the enemy came in and subverted it doesn't change that. It is the vehicle God designed for a husband and wife to come together in the way God wanted.

Everyone may be doing it, but God's design hasn't changed. It is an act meant for a husband and his wife. This is the first thing I need you to understand. The boundaries of sex are set within marriage, not outside of it. So, it doesn't matter if everyone is doing it. And by the way, that's not true. Some people are not doing it, and you can be one of them. Having sex outside marriage will definitely take you off track. You must understand that sex outside the confines of marriage and sin of any kind will affect your intimacy with God. That's what sin does. But can you get back on track? Most definitely.

You need to know that one of the enemy's tricks is shame. Once you have had sex or done something wrong, he plays it on the screen of your mind. He tells you that you are a bad person and

God doesn't love you anymore. This is so far from the truth. God hates sin, but He loves you, no matter what you do. The Bible says that while we were yet sinners, Christ died for us *(see Romans 5:8)*. He doesn't sit in heaven thinking, she is so bad now, and I don't love her anymore. When God sent Jesus, He knew we were messed up and needed saving. He made provisions way in advance, before we were even conceived. Shame is the enemy's trick of the trade, and it's the key to this particular detour. Think about it.

Have you wondered if God is repaying you for the things you did wrong? Have you thought, "God is punishing me for my past sins?" This is a well-used tactic of the enemy to keep you down, particularly with sexual sin. So, I will say it again: God loves you and is not punishing you for your past sins. Are there consequences for some of your actions? Yes, but that is a spiritual principle at work, not God sitting in heaven, doling out punishment. I know without a doubt that if you go to God and ask for mercy, even the consequences can change. Where you should receive judgement, mercy can and will be shown to you. Ask for it as it is yours for the taking. I am a testimony that you can come off this detour. If I was judged by my sexual past, I shouldn't have the relationship I have with God or the marriage I have today.

So, how do you get back on track? First of all, repent. To repent is a bit more than feeling sorrowful in heart and vowing not to do it again. It is to have a change of heart and to renew your thinking on the matter. I already started helping you with this when I said, "sex is good, but it is for marriage". That's the first thing you must do; understand what sex is and what the Bible says about it. This is the foundational revelation you must build on. Ask the Holy Spirit to give you a personal revelation of what sexual sin and sin of any kind can do. You must know what it can do to you and your relationship with God. I'll tell you this; when you have this revelation, it will change your attitude toward sex. You will make a quality decision, as Kenneth Copeland calls it. Like Daniel in the Bible, you won't want to defile yourself.

As you repent, you must break the soul tie(s) instituted when you had sex. I already said that having sex joins the husband and wife. Therefore, it is not a total break when you have sex with someone who isn't your husband, even if you break up with him. For a complete break, you must break the soul tie that "ties" you both together, and how else can you do that if not by first repenting?

Start by praying about it and asking God, through His Holy Spirit, to help you break free. If He leads you to fast about it, then pray and fast about it. Also, recognise that you have Jesus and your body is now the temple of the living God. Jesus made you free through His death and resurrection, so you are free from the soul tie(s). Knowing and accepting this truth is a big part of what will help you break free. If you are led to do so, you can confess what you did to a counsellor, trusted friend or your future spouse. The reason for this is so that the enemy doesn't keep you bound in shame through secrecy.

Part of your confession to yourself, at least, is to call the soul tie what it is; a soul tie. Not a relationship, a one-night stand or a fling but a soul tie. You can use a phrase like, "I have a soul tie with this person, and I am breaking free now." You might feel uncomfortable as you say it, but please just say it. Your words are powerful, and they can set you free. Finally, remove anything that reminds you of the person or persons you had sex with. This might include unfriending on social media or blocking their phone number. Get rid of sex toys and give away any presents they gave you. All these things are reminders of the soul tie(s), and you don't want them in your space anymore. The whole essence is to be free, and free you will be.

Once you have broken the soul tie, the next step is to set boundaries around sex. In this season, there will be many triggers for sex. A lot of it will be audio-visual. Protect your senses. Even now, as a married woman, I still protect my eyes and ears from sex. I skip sexual scenes on tv or change the channel. I did this a lot as a single woman, so I didn't get turned on by a sex scene on the screen. I would say that it is wise to do this. The same applies when you get into a relationship. Be careful what you watch with him, even when you are engaged. Don't stir sexual love before its time. You have many years to explore each other's bodies. And by the way, masturbation isn't exactly an option either. That is satisfying your sexual desire by yourself, which is also contrary to God's design.

Ask the Holy Spirit to help you grow in self-control. Self-control is a fruit of the Spirit. The more you grow your relationship with God, the more you will have self-control. On a practical level, find other wholesome activities to take your mind off the desire. You may need to change locations, leave the house, call a friend or do something else. The key is to arrest the train of thought and any later actions. If you have an ex, this is not the best time to call to say hi. That's playing with fire.

When you get into a relationship, have some ground rules. The first thing I always recommend is having an adult conversation about sex. The aim of this is not only for him to agree with you that sex is not on the cards but to ensure that you are both on the same wavelength when it comes to honouring God with your bodies. I'll never forget something my older sister told me when I turned twenty-one. She said I should look for a man who had a desire to please God, not me. If he desires to please God, he won't do anything to hurt you. He will always think about his actions and decisions in light of his relationship with God. This sex conversation is not one to shy away from. You are both adults, and this is an essential part of your relationship. It may be uncomfortable, but you need to have it.

Once you are on the same page, the next part of the conversation should be about the boundaries you both need to have. Boundaries ensure that you stick to your decision. The reason we end up having sex when we say we won't is because of this; a lack of boundaries. So here are some boundaries I would recommend.

Meet in public places. It sounds like a no-brainer, but you'll be amazed that it isn't obvious to many people. You are less likely to have sex if you are out and about in a shopping mall or taking a walk in the park. I know you want intimate conversations, but should they be at the cost of the decision you've made? You can find a quiet corner in a public place to have intimate, wholesome conversations. I say wholesome because intimacy doesn't only have to do with sex. You shouldn't be having sexually suggestive conversations anyway. Remember, you are trying not to arouse love before its time. Have conversations that help you know him more on other levels. You have many years ahead to have sexy conversations.

Then there's the "**no sleepovers**" boundary. Yes, I know you can sleep in separate rooms, but you must think beyond yourself. Apart from avoiding spaces where you can have sex, you are also removing the appearance of evil. What do I mean? An appearance of evil, as the Bible calls it, is when something looks evil, even if the actual incident or thing isn't. Sleeping over, even if you don't have sex, gives the appearance that you did. Someone looking from the outside can or may assume that you did. You know you didn't, but how can you prove that to them? You may say, what they think about you isn't your business. True, it isn't, but what impression does it give of you? How does that help you keep your honour and dignity as a woman? Food for thought.

Another boundary you can implement when you are in a relationship is **spending time with others**. They act as chaperones, preventing you from getting into any trouble.

Oh, and don't forget the boundary of **physical touch**. A question that many singles ask is, "How far can we go?" Here's my answer: As far as you would if your dad or Jesus was sitting in front of you! I doubt very much you would even kiss in front of your dad, talk less of any heavy petting. Now, imagine that the Holy Spirit is always with you and sees all you do. If He is important to you, like your dad is, I am sure you wouldn't want to do certain things in front of Him.

The final thing I would say is to put a boundary on **what you wear**. Men are visually stimulated. It is how they are. I know you want to keep him hot for you, but you can do so whilst looking good and covered. At least leave some things to the imagination at this stage. He doesn't need to know that you have all the right assets to keep him entertained. He will see much more in marriage, so why not wait till then?

Previous sexual activity and sins don't have to derail you on your journey to marriage. Yes, it is a detour, but you can get back on track as you take steps in the right direction. Don't let the enemy shame you into staying stuck. There is hope for you. I know this because I experienced it, and so can you.

Keep Moving

Detours aren't a destination. They are only a wrong turn along the journey. You must keep moving even when you have taken a detour. If I could navigate the detours I experienced and still get to my destination, so can you. It doesn't matter what the detour is, you can come back from it and still make it to your destination. I know detours can add time to a journey, but at the end of the day, God is a redeemer of time. What you think you have lost based on some of the experiences you have been through, God can redeem. It is His nature to redeem time and make all things work together for your good. The key thing is that you must get back on track.

However, I must ask, do you want to get back on track? I have to ask because we sometimes tie our identities to what we have been through. In doing so, we don't get to experience the better life waiting for us. Are you ready to let go of the version of yourself that these detours may have created? Are you ready to find the real you? If you are, fantastic.

If you think you can't change because this is who you are, I want you to know that is not true. You can let go of the false identity the detour(s) may have given you. Don't let a moment on any of these detours stop you from reaching your destination. Get up and clean up your act. Do what you need to do and refocus on the journey ahead. Your marriage awaits you.

Reflections

What did I already know that was affirmed in this chapter?

....

What new thing did I learn from this chapter?

....

What can I do with what I now know?

....

What example(s), if any, resonated with me and what didn't?

....

What have I learned that I can start doing right away?

....

Actions

Here are three things I will do based on what I learned in this chapter:

1..
....
2..
....
3..
....

10
The Compass

"Who you are determines who you will be with."
~ *Bunmi Oduah* ~

They say we learn in hindsight. I agree. When I look back on my journey, I see what God was doing all along, but I can't say I saw it when it was happening. I was sure it was the enemy stopping me from getting married. You may think the same. Growing up in the African culture, as I did, everything was the enemy's fault, and that enemy was not only the devil but also the people around us. It was a culture that conditioned us to think of people as our enemies.

Yes, I know, a strange way of thinking, right? We only have one enemy, the devil. Does he sometimes use individuals to dispatch his assignments? Yes, he does, but always remember that these people are being used as tools. More often than not, they don't have a clue what they are doing. Let's banish the ideology that people are our enemies; they aren't. When I see someone doing something wrong to me, it can hurt at first, but once I get over the initial hurt, it's easy to see that they are being used by the real enemy. That helps me have a heart that asks God to open their eyes so they can see.

Anyway, that was the mindset I had when I started my journey to marriage. Now, I realise it was less of the enemy delaying my marriage. It was more a combination of a few other things, with me being the biggest contributor. There was so much work I had to do as an individual, but I didn't think so at the time. I was sure that I was perfect and ready for marriage. I might have told God so a few times when I was demanding to get married. Looking back at my demands, I am glad He didn't answer me. I can't even begin to imagine the disaster my marriage would be today. I had some faulty thinking and understanding at the time.

Instead of answering me, God took me on a journey of transformation. He opened me up to knowledge and revelation that changed me. That's what I want to talk about in this chapter. It would not profit you to have waited this long to get married and still be the same woman. You must deal with "the little foxes that spoil the vine" *(see Song of Solomon 2:15)*. What do I mean? Let me share a bit of my background with you.

I grew up in Lagos, Nigeria and did my bachelor's degree at the University of Lagos. Things had started heating up in my generation and the ones after. Our appetites were expanding. I was in university at a time when we were being exposed to a lifestyle beyond our years. This lifestyle wasn't fit for someone just starting out in life. There were parties, outings and expenses for my older siblings, but it seemed there was nothing for someone my age. To put this in perspective, my older siblings are much older than me. I'm talking about living a lifestyle meant for forty-year-olds when you're in your twenties.

That was the kind of lifestyle I was exposed to then, and as a result, my appetite changed. I didn't want to date the boys on campus because I considered them to be, well, boys. I thought they couldn't afford the things I wanted. They were still interested in hanging out in clubs, drinking and driving fast cars. I wanted men who could afford lounges, upscale bars, and much more. Real men who were earning an income and didn't mind spoiling me. After all, my friends and roommates were being spoilt, and I wanted the same. But there was one challenge. My mum was a lecturer at my university, so I was a bit more popular than I wanted to be. It meant I couldn't always get away with the things I wanted to. It's also why I wanted to interact with guys who weren't in the university system. I didn't want tales filtering back to my mum.

But this came with its issues.

Interacting with the type of men I wanted to be with meant going to certain places where I would likely meet my older siblings, their friends or people who knew my family. Lagos is small like that. The dilemma of a girl who wants more than she should at her age. All this exposure started to shape how I viewed men and the kind of life I wanted. I still had this mindset when I met my ex-fiancé after graduating. I tempered my appetite to get the marriage I wanted because that was more important. Besides, he was earning an income and giving me some of the things I wanted anyway.

I gave my life to Christ whilst dating my ex-fiancé, but my mindset didn't change. If there is anything I have learnt, it is that giving your life to Jesus doesn't automatically change you. What it does do is give you access to all of heaven's resources and God, who can change you if you let Him. Unfortunately, I didn't do this at the time and continued my life with Jesus as an add-on. After my ex-fiancé and I broke up, I only gave my attention to guys who fit my preconceived model of the kind of man I wanted. If they didn't, I would let things fizzle out. I didn't want to "suffer" in marriage, and if the guy didn't look like he could look after me, what was the point?

I am still amazed at the woman God has made me today because I am not that girl anymore. I am not only amazed but also super thankful that I am not her anymore. My transformation is a testimony. It is one that I pray will bring others to know the God who changed me. I know it could only have been God who could unearth all that was dysfunctional in me at the time. He presented me with a higher truth that changed me. That change didn't happen overnight because, hey! I had many years of my background, environment, experiences and society at work in me.

Like you, I wasn't shaped in a day. Everything we have experienced and all that we've seen have shaped us into who we are today. My shaping had made me associate wealth in marriage with a particular type of man. Yours may have caused you to view a good life as something you must fight for at all costs because you don't want to be poor. Or you could view men based on how your father treated your mother when you were growing up.

Everything we experience is always pulling us in a direction. The question I often ask myself now is, what direction is that? With all that I am seeing and hearing, who am I becoming? That's a question you must ask yourself as you go through life. You don't want to look back years from now and wonder how you got there. You want to be who God planned for you to be. Not only that, but with the people He planned for you to be there with, doing what He planned for you to do. So, with that question in mind, let us talk about the compass.

A compass is a tool to help you navigate your way in a particular direction or geographical location. When people go walking in the woods, for example, they usually have a map and compass so they don't get lost. Any activity that requires navigation or finding direction will usually need a compass. The compass helps you stay on the right path to the destination you want to get to.

On the journey to marriage, I want you to realise that you have a compass for getting there. That compass is you. Let me help you understand what I mean. The woman you are on your journey is the compass that determines if you will get to your destination or not. So, in a nutshell, where you end up is determined by who you are.

If you, the compass, are faulty or don't have the right components, you are on the back foot. Your chances of getting to your desired destination, a marriage, that is, are slim. If you make it to your marriage, it may not be the kind you want. It could be so bad that you may have to walk away. Who you are, as a person, matters a lot when it comes to what you will get when it comes to marriage.

As a compass has many parts, so do you as a woman. You are a multi-layered woman, made up of different parts that create the masterpiece you are. I know you may look at yourself right now and not see a masterpiece, but in God's eyes, you are a masterpiece. Everything He is doing in you or allowing you to go through is shaping you into His finished work.

That is why it is so important for you to look at yourself holistically and ask an important question. "Am I all I am supposed to be, or is there more?" This is not a self-deprecating review, far from it. Instead, this review helps you see the areas where you can still evolve. It's not a "What is wrong with me?" look at yourself, but a "Is there more I can become?" one. The two are in no way the same. The first looks at you through a negative lens, while the other is through a positive one. Even when you're married, you must keep asking yourself the second question. As we keep growing in age, we must also keep evolving because our evolution isn't a one-time event.

Reflecting on my journey, I now see that I have evolved over several years. Yours may not be years; it could be months or even weeks. It all depends on how you respond to the transformation journey God wants and will take you on. I didn't respond immediately as I was too focused on getting married and how I was coming up short on that goal. It was only when I surrendered to my process, as I mentioned earlier, that things began to take shape.

Don't be like me and drag out this journey any longer than it needs to be. God can redeem the time, but I would prefer it if you flowed with Him so that He doesn't have to redeem time on your behalf. Let Him transform you into the woman He has destined you to be so you can attract your husband. When I say attract, I don't mean a physical attraction. I am talking about how God makes you into the woman your husband can recognise and want to be with. Your husband has a picture of the wife he wants to be with, and God is making you into that woman. It's what happened when Adam saw

Eve. Why do you think he was not confused about who she was? I believe it was because she embodied everything he knew he was looking for in a helper. So, when he saw her, it clicked. That's how it is supposed to be with you and your husband.

So, what makes up your compass? Your identity, your character, your mindset and your purpose.

Identity

Have you noticed that royals tend to marry royals or people of royal blood? Why do you think that is? There are several reasons, but from our perspective in this book, I would like you to consider this. There is a common background and lifestyle that they are all accustomed to. Now, think of yourself as the daughter of the King. Should you marry someone who isn't a royal? I am not advocating being a snob; I am talking more about the compatibility of identities. A princess usually marries a prince. I know writers worldwide have glamorised the story of the royal who gave it all up. The royal gave up everything for the love of someone who wasn't royalty. It all sounds sweet and romantic. They usually don't tell you the inner workings of such a relationship. When the relationship works, it is usually because both parties have put in so much to make it happen. And when it doesn't, the cause is usually the differences in their identities.

As a daughter of the King, God, you should seek to find His son. You should desire a prince who is aware of his royal lineage and takes it seriously. Don't let the desire to get married make you drop your crown for someone who does not value your lineage. The challenges of being with someone who isn't like you are not insurmountable. Even though they aren't, why climb a mountain if you don't have to? Why embark on the difficult task of trying to make a relationship that wasn't meant to be, work?
Growing your relationship with God will help you stay rooted in your royal identity. God has a vested interest in seeing you become

who He made you. He will always remind you of your identity as His daughter. As you do so, you will become more confident in who you are. This confidence will drive away those who don't have a similar identity. Please don't feel bad when this happens; it is a good thing. After all, you don't want to be with a man with the wrong identity.

The truth is when it comes to identity, a godly woman will attract a godly man. I'd say it's a natural affinity. Please don't fall for the saying that opposites attract because they can later attack. I can hear someone say, "Bunmi, that is not true." Before you protest, let me tell you something you may not know. The godly women you see and know who married ungodly men gave up their crowns. If you had an honest conversation with them, they just might tell you the truth. How they thought they could cope with his "*surface*" godliness or how they hoped to change him. The second reason is usually why such mismatched relationships happen: It is not any woman's responsibility to change a man! You are not the Holy Spirit; changing the man is the man's responsibility. I say all this to encourage you to stand in your identity as the daughter of the King. Believe that His son, a prince worthy of you, will find you.

The best way to know who you are is to know whose you are. The Word of God is full of information about your identity. The New Testament is a great place to find out who you are. For example, you are the righteousness of God in Christ Jesus. You don't need to do anything to be righteous, apart from giving your life to Him. Being righteous means you can speak to God freely, and all the hosts of heaven want to support you. You are no longer a sinner but a saint. Christ gave you a new identity, and that identity is always right with God. This isn't a liberty to sin but for you to know that you are free from the weight of religion - no more theatrics to win God's favour. Your place as His righteous daughter means you are favoured.

Another way I learned about my identity was by knowing that

there was a spiritual character in the Bible like me. We all have a Bible character like us, and mine is Deborah, the first female judge of Israel. There was something about her that drew me in. One day, I did a study on her, and I had a light bulb moment. Reading about her felt like I was reading about myself. She reminded me of me. The same applies to you too. There is a spiritual character in the Bible that is almost a prototype of who you are. You may not know who they are today. It might take you some time, but I can bet that now you've read this, you will desire to know yours. You are likely to start seeing who they are; when you read your Bible, that is. The easiest way to answer this question is to ask yourself, "who am I most like in the Bible?" Which character have I always liked? Then trust the Holy Spirit to lead you on a journey of discovery as you read your Bible.

Even your name, the name your parents gave you, is a clue to your identity. My full name is Olubunmi, a Yoruba name which means God's gift. For many years, I didn't think that I was a gift. In time, I realised that I am a gift, and my presence is a gift to others. Now, I embody my name, conscious that I am a gift. The more people call my name, the more they declare that I am a gift. If you don't know the meaning of your name, I would encourage you to find out. Your name is linked to your identity. There's a reason your parents gave you that name. It may be tied to what was happening at your conception and birth. Learning the meaning of your name may give you a sense of why you are the way you are. If your name has a negative meaning or doesn't seem to carry any particular meaning, you may want to change it or start using your other name. Your identity is too important for you not to know some of these things I am sharing with you.

As you go on your identity discovery journey, you will learn about your personality. Please know this; you are a woman with a personality and a certain type of temperament. You were created in the image of God with a personality to go with your spiritual identity. Whether you're an introvert, an extrovert, or a mix of both, you must know. You could be someone whose head rules over their heart or vice versa. Understanding your personality and temperament will help you appreciate how you are wired. It would also help you know why you may struggle with certain people, including certain men. Several personality assessments can help you understand your personality. Two great ones are the DiSC and Myers-Briggs assessment. Take them. You might be surprised how true to type the results are. Let what you learn about yourself guide you, not restrict you.

As you may have gathered, the journey of identity discovery is so important. When you know who you are, you will know who you can and should be with for the rest of your life. You are less likely to accommodate a man who does not value who you are and mistreats you. The more aware I became of who I was, the less I entertained certain men. Like I said earlier, it was not because I was proud; far from it. I knew I was worthy of the best kind of love and affection a man could give; I deserved a man who knew and valued my worth.

As you read this, I want to encourage you to make an effort to know who you are. Spend time in the word of God and see what He says about you. Let His words about you keep you grounded even on this journey to marriage. If you want a constant reminder, write out words that describe you on a card you keep with you all the time. If you like technology, you can even create a screensaver of your identity. That way, whenever you pick up your phone, you get a reminder of who you are.

Character

I was recently sharing with some ladies about the importance of character. I shared that character is what you live with for the rest of your life. He might do nice things before he marries you, but his character is what you will live with for the rest of your life. It's the same for him; he gets to live with your character daily. I remember a guy I dated many years ago who told me something I still have not forgotten. He said, "there's only so long people can pretend for. It is usually about a year." In our conversation about what he said, I understood that your character does not hide for long. In time, your values, morals and the resulting behaviour will show, no matter how hard you try.

Reflecting on my life so far, he was right. Our true nature cannot stay hidden. When life happens, and it will, our character shows itself, whether good or bad. Many years ago, I posted about marriage revealing our true nature. I had not been married very long then, but my marriage had started showing me who I was. When I shared this online, I had people who agreed and those who didn't; most of those who didn't were single and, in my opinion, wearing rose-tinted glasses.

As a younger lady, I remember being told that I had to stop being lazy because no man would marry me if I continued being that way. Ouch! It hurt at the time, and it took the Holy Spirit doing a deep work to wipe the pain of such words from my heart. But, as much as the words were painful and could have been said more lovingly, the truth was that I was lazy. I say was because I am no longer that young lady anymore, and I am on a journey to being more like who God wants me to be. Still not perfect, but not who I was. Thank Jesus for that because I am not sure my husband would have been able to cope!

The journey to marriage is a great time to look at your character in the mirror and ask yourself some deep, soul-searching questions. Questions like "What is my character like?", "What do those close to me say about me?", "Where do I need to either change or improve?" As I became more self-aware on the journey to marriage, I had to put up a mirror and face the uncomfortable truth about that part of my character.

Character is what people see. It is who we are when the chips are down. People judge us based on their interaction with our character, whether we present our true character or not. Your character matters. It is why God is taking you through this season, to refine your character, not to punish you but to bless you and who you end up marrying. I am thankful for many things that happened to me on my marriage journey, but refining my character is one of the things I'm most grateful to God for.

In Galatians 5:22-23, there is a list of character qualities we should all have as children of God. The scriptures are filled with godly character qualities such as faithfulness, kindness, love, joy, integrity, honesty, and self-control, amongst many others. Unfortunately, most of us lack these qualities, mainly because of our upbringing or life experiences. I know I was sorely lacking in godly qualities. God knew that too, and started taking me through these circumstances that would bring out what was really in me. As He did, He would lovingly steer my heart to see the qualities in me that were not in line with His Word.

Some negative character traits I had to confront were impatience, envy and laziness. Interaction with people continually pulled out these traits; I could not escape my character. At first, I would blame the other person and not take responsibility for my behaviour. As far as I was concerned, it was them, not me. It takes a level of maturity to admit that your character and the resulting behaviour need work. Most times, we shy away from doing this because we feel ashamed. We don't want to appear as if we are weak, and we also wonder what people will say.

The truth is people will always have something to say. Don't let that stop you from embracing your character or working on the areas God has highlighted. It's not about them; it's about you and the woman you are to become. Working on your character will take time. You'll have moments when you are doing well and times when you will go off the rails. This is normal, and if you do fall, please don't think you're a failure or that you cannot continue. Falling shows that you're human. Picking yourself up and continuing to grow into the woman God wants is your divinity shining through.

The more you flow with God on your journey of character refinement, the more you will become the woman He wants. You'll see that your morals won't waver in the face of opposition or temptation. People will start to describe you based on your morals and great character. Not because you told them about it, but because they can see it in the way you now live and interact with them.

You've got all that it takes to become who God wants you to be character-wise. The host of heaven is rooting for you, Jesus is praying for you, and the Holy Spirit is always there to lend a helping hand.

Mindset

There is a verse in the book of Proverbs that has changed the way I view the human mind. It is Proverbs 23:7a which says, *"For as he thinks in his heart, so is he."* As a single woman, I was not aware of the power of my mind. I would even go as far as to say I was pretty clueless. Even when I started my journey of self-discovery, I still did not know how powerful my mind was.

I read my Bible and spoke declarations about the life I wanted and the woman I wanted to be. Even though I was renewing my mind as I did so, I did not know much about the mind. No wonder it took me so long to get married. Apart from my identity and character, my mind, which made up a big part of me, remained an area I was clueless about. I was already married when I fully understood the power of my mind. No one had articulated the part it played in the life that I was living. But God, being merciful, was working on my mind even on my journey from Miss to Mrs.

When I look back on the transformation that happened to me,

I realise that God did a deep work on my mind. First, he pulled up faulty beliefs and showed me the impact of my background and upbringing. Then He replaced them with the right beliefs using knowledge from the Bible. In hindsight, I realise that God did some mindset reengineering on me. He elevated my mind to become the magnet that could attract the marriage I desired.

Yes, your mind is like a magnet. It can attract or repel what you desire. If your mind has the right beliefs, especially about marriage, you will attract the right man. The same applies if your mind is full of faulty beliefs. That is how powerful your mind is and why you should pay a lot of attention to what you feed it.

If your mind has unhealthy content, it will produce unhealthy experiences. The same is true if your mind has healthy content. You may think your experiences are external to you, but that is not true. The truth is your mind has a big part to play in what you experience in life. Your mind houses your beliefs and your emotions. These shape your reasoning and decision-making. Your reasoning impacts the actions you take. Your actions produce the experiences you have. Can you see how they are all linked? What you believe will influence your emotions about whatever happens to you. Why? Because your beliefs are like a filter that triggers specific emotional responses. These emotions then influence your reasoning. They cause you to make choices and decisions in a certain way that produces the experience you have. Can you see how powerful your mind is?

Let me share an example that might help drive this home. Take the example of a little girl who was always rejected by her father whenever she failed a task. He only ever praised her when she excelled. The rejection hurt, but being a child, she made every effort to please her father. Guess what? She grew up to become an overachiever. In her mind, praise and achievement went hand-in-hand. She also viewed love through the lens of praise. One day, she met a man who didn't know about her background. He didn't praise her as she expected, so she believed he didn't love her. As you might guess, this caused issues in their relationship, and she ultimately broke up with him.

She goes into her next relationship, and the same thing happens. The cycle keeps repeating itself, and in time, she becomes disillusioned with men. Eventually, she goes to see a counsellor for help. The counsellor is trained to identify faulty beliefs and their impact. When the lady tells her story, the counsellor sees exactly what the problem is. As time goes by, with the counsellor's help, the lady realises that it was not that the men she met didn't love her. Instead, she was the one with the wrong definition of what love was. Her mind had taken the information of her past and settled it as a belief of how men were. This influenced her emotions, reasoning and decisions about her relationships.

As humans, we must constantly check our beliefs. Our beliefs drive what we experience in life. When we were born, we came as a blank canvas that people, starting with our parents, painted on. In time, we picked up beliefs and ideologies from them. As we went through life, society, via the news, social media, and church, all added their views. Then we experienced interpersonal relationships, especially with the opposite sex. That added another layer of beliefs based on what we experienced.

It can seem like a never-ending cycle, where our minds become a dumping ground, and we don't get to stop what happens to us. But that isn't true. We can prevent this from happening, that is, our minds being a dumping ground. Our thoughts reveal our beliefs. If we take intentional action, we can take control of our minds. It may sound hard, but it isn't. Let me share a personal example to help you see what I mean.

When I was pregnant with my son, I had to take control of my mind. At twenty-two weeks pregnant, I had a scare. My cervix opened, and I could have lost the pregnancy. Even after the doctors had fixed what was wrong, I still had this constant fear of losing him. I began to have physical symptoms. The fear started to affect my body. Then, after one more episode of being overwhelmed by the fear, I said, "No more." Remember what I said about how powerful our minds are?

It got to a point where I was tired of being afraid. As I asked God for help, He told me to focus on His word and take control of my thoughts. The next time I had a fearful thought about losing him, I would say, "No." Then I would declare what the scriptures said about my baby and me getting to full term. Whenever thoughts arose in my mind from a place of fear, I would stop them with the word "no". Then I would say what the word of God said about my baby and me.

"No" is such a powerful word, and you can use it too. In time, I was no longer fearful and had mastered my thoughts in that particular area. You can do the same about your thoughts about men and marriage.

To enjoy this waiting season and get married, you must check your beliefs. Where have they come from, and are they helping you or getting in your way? You will need to spend some time reflecting and reviewing your life. Pay attention to your experiences and see what beliefs have come from them. Here are some reflective questions to help you on this journey:

- What picture did your parents show you of marriage when you were growing up?
- What was your father like as a man, and how did he treat your mother?
- What common phrases did your mother use about your father and her marriage to him?
- What other familial influences (such as aunties and cousins) shaped your beliefs?
- What patterns did you notice in your previous relationships, and

what conclusions can you draw from them?
- What common sayings have you heard about men and marriage?
- What do you and your friends say about men and marriage when you talk?
- What views did you get about men and marriage through church and religion?

When you reflect and ask yourself these questions, don't shy away from the answers. Not all the answers will be negative. Some of what has shaped your belief will be positive. Embrace the positives as they are a good foundation. Then work on replacing the not-so-positive beliefs with the right ones.

You should reflect on where you are coming from because the answers are a window to your beliefs. If your beliefs are negative and don't align with God's word, then you must make an effort to change them. First, find scriptures in the Bible about the right qualities in men and marriage. Then, spend time reading and meditating on them. Let them become the picture that shapes your beliefs. That's how you begin to change your beliefs.

Your beliefs can change. You need to feed your mind with new, improved information and what better source for that than the word of God? The word of God is full of the highest level of information that can transform anyone. So, spend time with it. Look for what it says, especially about the qualities of a good husband and marriage. Trust me; it has plenty to say on this topic.

If you are going to become a magnet that attracts the right man, then make the effort to work on your beliefs. A godly woman with the right mindset will attract a godly man.

Purpose
"I am looking for my purpose" is a statement I hear very often. Once you bring up the topic of purpose, people tend to go into "I

know my purpose" or "I am looking for my purpose" mode. These are the two general camps, but there is a third camp which is much smaller. A camp of people who are not looking for their purpose. They know and are serving God's purpose for their lives. When you focus on "your purpose," you are more likely to think it is all about you. Our life's purpose was never about us. It has always been about the Purpose Giver, God.

God is the One who created every single one of us for His purpose. That is what we should be looking for; His purpose for our lives! Seeking out His purpose is less stressful than trying to find your purpose. To do so will require you to have a relationship with Him. If you want to know the purpose of anything, ask the person who created it. The same applies to us as God's daughters. If we want to know His purpose for our lives, we must ask Him. The relationship part makes it easier for us to hear Him when He does tell us. It also allows us to trust Him when the instructions that come with the purpose don't make sense. Can you see the importance of building a personal relationship with God? This is why I keep yakking on about it.

A relationship with God is the foundation of everything. This includes knowing the purpose for which God created you. The closer you are to God, the more likely He will reveal why He created you. Further, He will show you how He wants you to fulfil His purpose for your life. So, if you skimmed over the chapter on a relationship with God or aren't growing yours yet, I hope this motivates you.

A woman living in and on purpose is attractive. There is a vibe she gives off that draws others to her. People want to know what makes her glow, what makes her tick. Walking in God's purpose makes people gravitate toward you. When you are doing what God wants you to do, at the right place and time, I can tell you that your husband will find you. Why? Not only because you are attractive but also because you will be in the place of your assignment. God always blesses us when we're in the place of our assignment.

A good way to understand your purpose is to picture a jigsaw puzzle. Every piece in a jigsaw puzzle has been made to fit with other pieces and ultimately make the final picture. The edges of each piece are shaped to fit the next. As the pieces come together, we begin to see the image on the box. A piece cannot be forced to join with other pieces. Forcing won't make it fit; instead, it will damage the pieces around it.

Now take that picture and think of human beings. Humans are all pieces in God's giant puzzle. He has shaped every single one of us so we can slot into our place. Every part of our make-up was created to ensure we serve His purpose for our lives. When we begin to understand His purpose and live it out, we slot into our place in the bigger picture. Trying to copy another person's purpose is like forcing a piece of the puzzle into the wrong position. As I said earlier, you'll most likely damage those around you.

This is why it is so important to stay close to God and discover your purpose within the bigger plan. Then go after it with tunnel vision, not looking to the left or right. If you take your gaze off your purpose and focus on another's, you will get distracted. Your focus will shift to what was never meant to be your assignment. You are also likely to leave those you should serve, chasing after those you weren't. This is a recipe for frustration.

By the way, purpose applies to all works of life, not only entrepreneurship or ministry. I felt I had to say that as it is easy to think once you know your purpose, you should quit your day job. God wants to fulfil His purpose in every sphere of society. He wants to use us as entrepreneurs, pastors, bankers or social justice activists. As you seek God's purpose for your life, you should ask Him if you are already where you need to be. That way, you are less likely to quit your day job. For all you know, you might be exactly where He needs you to be.

Also, don't be too hard on yourself on this purpose journey. Not everyone wakes up and immediately knows what God created them to do. Sometimes, it takes years to even realise what purpose is all about. Others are blessed to have parents who help them follow their purpose early in life. If you are in the former camp, I want to encourage you with the words God spoke to me one day when I wept on my kitchen floor. That day was a climax of many days of wondering why I was just beginning to understand God's call on my life. I was feeling sorry for myself over the many years I had lost. In my mind, all the years with the various degrees and work experience seemed like a waste.

As I knelt on the kitchen floor weeping, I felt like I was playing catch up with my life, and it didn't seem fair. All the signs of God's call were evident when I reflected on my childhood to that point. Yet, here I was playing catch up. I poured out my heart with tear-filled eyes. God replied, "I can redeem time and give you the harvest of ten years in one year." Those words stopped my tears in their tracks, and peace came over me almost immediately.

It doesn't matter if you are late to your purpose party. God has been waiting for you with His ability to shorten the time you think you have lost. He can give you all you should have achieved in the shortest possible time. The key is to obey whatever He tells you to do on the journey.

The final thing I would say is that God's purpose for your life is always knocking on the door of your heart. It is knocking through the societal ills that frustrate you, experiences you have been through and gifts that flow through you. I have always loved relationships, especially between a man and a woman. From a young age, I read books about love relationships; not all godly, though. As a single woman, you would find me listening to a podcast or message about relationships on my way to and from work. I was always advising my friends about their relationships and personal development. I wasn't married, by the way.

After being married for some months, I started to feel unsettled. Marriage did not fill the hole made for my purpose. For clarity on what to do next, I joined a coaching mastermind. When asked what I would do if I didn't have to think about money, the words popped out of my mouth. "I'll help women in their relationships, so they don't make the same mistakes I made. There's no need for them to struggle." My life's purpose was popping out and answering what seemed like a simple question. Once I said those words, I knew that I had to do something about it. It was the only way I could fill the hole in me that was calling to be filled. Maybe purpose has been knocking on the door of your heart, and you didn't know it. Well, today, I want to encourage you to answer. Here is a prayer that can get you started.

"Father in heaven, you created me for Your purpose. Reveal to me why You created me and what You prepared for me to do before I was even born. Show me how to walk in Your purpose for my life using the gifts that come to me naturally. Connect me to the people I am meant to serve and let Your name be glorified in Jesus' name, amen."

As you pray, pay attention to the problems you feel like solving. Take note of the gifts, talents and passions you become more aware of. Think of the experiences you've been through and the things that hurt your heart. Begin to dream of the life you want to live. These are all-purpose linked. Pay attention!

There Are No Shortcuts

The truth is that there is no shortcut to a kingdom marriage. I wish there were. If it existed and I knew it, I'd tell you in a heartbeat. You are the compass that will guide you to the marriage that honours God. Your spirituality and prayers are an excellent foundation, but they are not a shortcut. Sorry to burst your bubble on that one. Prayer cannot act as a shortcut for a faulty compass. God's hands are tied when we don't become who He wants us to be, as He is bound by the principles and laws of the kingdom.

Don't get mad at God for not giving you the marriage you desire if you have not become the woman for that marriage. Too often, we get angry at God for not giving us our desired marriage. Can you remember what I mentioned earlier about God's process of maturation? God is not slack about His promises. One thing He has made clear to me over the years regarding marriage is that He can connect spouses in a heartbeat. That's an easy thing for Him to do. His concern is whether we are fit to handle the marriage He has for us. That's the bigger picture.

Think about it. If you had a child right now, would you hand them the keys to your car without ensuring they could drive? Wouldn't that be a recipe for disaster or an accident waiting to happen? It is the same with God. When He looks at you and me, He always sees the bigger picture. He sees so much more than we can. I can imagine Him asking Himself questions He already knows the answer to. Questions like "Can my daughter handle what I want to give her?" If He doesn't believe so, He will continue working on you until you can handle what He has for you. That's why He keeps tugging on your heart and tapping your shoulder. He is trying to show you the higher version of yourself that your marriage requires.

The ultimate question is, "Will you respond to His promptings and become that woman?"

Reflections

What did I already know that was affirmed in this chapter?
....

What new thing did I learn from this chapter?
....

What can I do with what I now know?
....

What example(s), if any, resonated with me and what didn't?
....

What have I learned that I can start doing right away?
....

Actions

Here are three things I will do based on what I learned in this chapter:

1..
....
2..
....
3..
....

11
Wife in Waiting

"When a man has found a wife, he has found a treasure! She is the gift of God to bring him joy and pleasure…"
~ ***Proverbs 18:22 (TPT)*** ~

"Your husband won't eat indomie noodles or drink garri. Is that what you will offer him when he gets back from work?"

Those were the words my mother often told me when I lived at home in Nigeria. Being her first daughter, I know she had (probably still does) high expectations for me. Let's say that due to my somewhat rebellious streak, I did not make things easy for her. Yet, you would never guess if you met me. I do not like being controlled or boxed in, but that's how I felt when I was younger.

Growing up, I hated being told what to do and how to toe the line of the perfect child. Looking back now, I realise that it was not that I loved being rebellious. I didn't fit the prescribed mould for me, and the only way to respond was to kick against it. Now that I am older and more self-aware, I know it was the non-conformist in me struggling. I struggled to fit into the conventional description of who I should be. Whether that was as a woman, daughter or one born into the society that I was.

My mum meant well. I know that now. She wanted the best for me, and I didn't look like I was heading in the right direction. Now that I am a mother, I understand how she felt, and my children aren't even teenagers yet. I also understand that she had been given a script by society on how to raise a child. Remember the script from earlier? The one that doesn't consider your unique strengths, weaknesses or destiny? Yeah, that one.

Based on culture, tradition and societal norms, I had to be able to do certain things to be the "perfect" wife. You can bet that cooking, cleaning, and generally knowing how to keep a house were top of the list. Unfortunately, those were things I didn't particularly like doing at the time. I'm still not too fond of cleaning, but that's by the side. Imagine my mother's frustration with this child of hers. I didn't want to participate in house chores and wasn't inclined to spend hours in the kitchen.

I was looking for the easiest way out when it came to all that. Hence her constant phrase about the food I would feed my husband when I got married. I'll let you know that he hasn't been drinking garri (cassava flakes) but has eaten Indomie noodles. He has even requested it on occasion. I make the most excellent Indomie noodle dish, if I say so myself, but I digress. My point is that what she feared never came to pass.

By the time I met my husband, I had been single for several years and had become a wife. Yes, you heard me say it; I had become a wife. You may be wondering what I mean by that. That's what this whole chapter is about. How does one become a wife whilst still single? Simple; by preparation. That preparation isn't only knowing how to cook rice in twenty different ways or ironing a shirt.

You can become a wife whilst single, and I know this for a fact. "He who finds a wife, finds a good thing and obtains favour from the Lord" (Proverbs 18:22). It is about becoming a wife, even in this season. You don't have to wait till you sign the dotted lines on your wedding day to become a wife. That's only a stamp, legalising your union. In God's kingdom, being a wife starts way before that.

I'll let you in on an insight the Holy Spirit opened my eyes to see. This was later confirmed by my husband. When your husband meets you, he looks at you through the lens of a wife. Notice I said husband and not a boyfriend. A man who wants to get married is looking for a wife. He isn't only looking for a woman who will warm his bed and fill his belly. He is sizing you up against what he wants. In his mind, he is wondering whether you can fulfil his emotional needs. Will you care for his extended family and help him become the man he wants to be? These are some of the questions uppermost in his mind. He is not seeing a woman; he is seeing a wife. Thinking that the wife part comes after the wedding ceremony will only frustrate you. For him, it comes before.

Now don't get me wrong. I am not asking you to start pretending to be a wife; far from it. I often tell single women not to give away wifely privileges to men who aren't committed to them. That is a recipe for heartbreak. I know this because I did it for several years. After another failed relationship, I finally stopped. It was as though I had a eureka moment. Doing the wifely things and playing house didn't make the guys I was dating commit to me.

You may say, "But how will I show him I can be the wife he needs?" I'll tell you this, "It is not by cooking and cleaning for him every weekend or setting up home at his place." I remember joking that my husband was eating fine before meeting me, so he didn't need me to sort out his meals. He had somehow survived before he met me, so a few more months wouldn't hurt. Now, this doesn't mean he didn't taste my cooking when we were courting. He did, but it was not regular practice to set up shop in his kitchen at the weekends or stock his fridge for him.

When he visited me, he ate like a king. I made sure of that. On those occasions, he got an insight into my cooking skills. Yes, I learnt to cook years after my mum's nagging and found out I loved doing it. I just didn't like cooking under compulsion. Sorry, mummy! You can show you are hospitable by showing your hospitality when he visits you. It is not a contest. Be yourself and let him see you for who you are. That's who he will live with for the rest of his life, not the woman you pretend to be. I've already said that you become a wife way before signing the register on your wedding day. I know that may sound confusing but stick with me.

Being a wife starts with what you do today, not what you will do in your marriage. It is in who you are right now; **emotionally, mentally, financially, socially and physically.** We often put off things we should do right now with the notion that we will somehow know how to do them in marriage. If only that were true. There's no magic switch to flick on the day you sign the dotted lines. This is why your single season is so important when preparing for the marriage you desire.

Marriage already has its challenges. Anyone who tells you otherwise is doing you a disservice. Meshing the lives of two people who aren't family members comes with its challenges. However, those challenges can be cut in half or reduced when you use your single season to prepare for it. Your life today is a trial run for your life of tomorrow. That's the truth. Everything you do today sets you up for tomorrow, good or bad. So, you might as well choose the good.

Choosing the good means becoming who you want to be in your marriage today, not tomorrow. It will need you to intentionally choose to become a wife. You can do this by using your current relationships and interactions to practice. For example, if you want to be a hospitable hostess as a wife, be hospitable now with your family and friends. If you want to be a loyal wife to your husband, be loyal to your friends now. Do you catch my drift?

Your current relationships allow you to be a wife long before you say, "I do." As I said, they are a trial run for the future you dream of. You might as well embrace them, knowing that how you handle them is a glimpse into the wife you will be when you marry. Notice I said when not if, because I am convinced beyond a shadow of a doubt that marriage is possible for you. We're not all like Apostle Paul or Jesus, who remained unmarried. They were the exception, not the rule. Most of the heroes of Christianity, including those in the hall of fame in the book of Hebrews chapter eleven, were married.

Now that we have settled that let us focus on five key areas you need to work on to become a wife.

An Emotionally Secure Wife in Waiting

I remember when I first drove a car with the lane departure feature. Every time I went over the lines for the lane without indicating, I would hear a beeping sound. That beeping sound was my cue to get back in lane and stop drifting. We have the same with our emotions. They usually point to something, good or bad. They tell us when things are going well and not so well.

Over the years, it has become clear to me that we aren't always great with our emotions. Sometimes, we let them lead us down unhealthy paths. We chase the high of feel-good emotions and bury or ignore the "down in the dump" ones. We forget that life is full of highs and lows with many plateaus. It doesn't help that most of us weren't taught how to manage our emotions. Not as part of the standard school curriculum or our general upbringing do we get told what to do. We are just expected to know how to manage our emotions.

It is no wonder that many of us struggle with our emotions, be it articulating our feelings or how to manage them. Yet, if you are going to be the wife your husband needs, you will need to pay attention to your emotions. You will need to recognise the emotions you are feeling and how to manage them. For example, you may see the picture of a married couple looking happy and start feeling sad. That photo was a trigger, and the feeling of sadness was your response. It could be that the image triggered thoughts of disappointment and dejection.

When I am triggered by something, I have learnt to ask myself a simple question: "Why are you triggered by this?" Such a simple question but one that helps me understand and manage my emotions. It does require reflection and sometimes facing uncomfortable truths. I know that I have had to face some uncomfortable truths when I have asked myself this question. You must query your emotions when you feel them, especially the negative ones. To query, in this case, is to dig beneath the surface of your feelings and get to the root cause.

I try to do this when my emotions are all over the place. I know that if I don't know the root cause, I can't deal with what I am feeling. So this is how I get started with my reflection. First, "Why do I feel this way?" Then, when I know the why, I ask myself, "What is it that made me feel the way I do?" The answer may also point to a who, "Who made me feel this way?", "What about them, or my interaction with them, caused these emotions to rise?" This will eventually lead to "What can I or should I do about these emotions?"

I can tell you that the more you do this, the more intelligent you will be with your emotions. Not only that, but it will help you thrive more as a person as you become more self-aware. You are in charge of how you feel, no matter what the trigger may be. Your emotions are within your control, and managing them is too. This will be an essential skill in marriage as there will be days when your spouse may trigger you. So, start building it today.

Apart from your feelings, you must also deal with any emotional baggage you may have. Emotional baggage is a big deal as it can make or mar your marriage in the future. Many marriages today suffer from untreated emotional baggage from both parties. It's not only women who have emotional baggage. Men do too. The emotional baggage people are dealing with varies. We all have something we are carrying around. This season is a great time to work through whatever that baggage may be. You need to focus mainly on the ones that may affect your marriage.

Your emotional baggage may be from an absent father, an abusive home or even a broken heart. Whatever it may be, I want to encourage you to stop running from it. It is time to heal. Turn towards it. Face it. Acknowledge what it did to you. Seek professional help if you don't know how to deal with it. Please don't bring this burden into your marriage.

Work to become an emotionally whole woman because that's who you are meant to be. You may be a successful woman, and everyone thinks you have it all together. Yet, you know there are places within you where you hurt. Aren't you tired of hurting? Don't you want to be healed? Even if your past has defined you, you don't have to keep that identity. I know it may get you sympathy which you've come to enjoy, but it isn't healthy. It won't help your marriage, especially if your husband doesn't pander to it.

Don't let your past affect your present or future. Your healing is so important. It will prevent you from making the wrong choice because your pain won't be a filter through which you view men and marriage. I especially want you to think about your childhood and work through any pain or trauma you experienced. Why? Because those are the most impressionable years of our lives. What we experienced in those years tends to leave an indelible mark.

Also, focus on your fathering or the lack of it. A woman's first glimpse of a man is her father. His presence, absence, character and behaviour mean a lot as it shapes how she views men. If her father mistreats women, it leaves its mark on her psyche. The same applies if he treats women well. Here are some questions I would like you to answer.

What picture did your father show you of a man?

How did he treat your mum?

How did he relate to you and your siblings, if you have any?

What was his character like?

I ask these questions because you may not know the childhood emotional baggage you carry. Could it be the reason why you are withdrawn and distrusting of men? It might be your father, and not your past relationships, who is to blame. Earlier in this book, I showed you what can happen when a father treats his daughter poorly and how his behaviour can shape her mindset and affect her actions and experiences. What I didn't go into are the wounds created by the experience - her constant validation-seeking from a man or the effect on the kind of wife she might become. What I didn't share was how it distorted her definition of love. How as an adult, she couldn't receive love from either God or a good man because she didn't recognise what true love was. Yet, God wants to heal that wound. He wants to remind her that He loves her, not because of anything she does or doesn't do but because she is His. He also wants to do the same for you.

If you have experienced hurt in a previous relationship and haven't healed, then that is trauma. It can have long-term effects if left untreated. That's why I wrote the chapters on "Detours and Reroutes." If you skimmed over them, please go back. Immerse yourself in them and follow the action steps.

You may have heard the phrase "hurt people hurt people." When we don't heal from emotional trauma, whether great or small, we may end up hurting those around us. It is not intentional. It is just how we have become wired. We may not even realise what we're doing as it has become normal. Emotional baggage is sneaky like that. Not only can it cause you to hurt others, but it can also make you put pressure on the man in your life. It can make you ask him to fill a hole he was not designed to fill. Filling that hole is God's and your responsibility. As you turn to God in your relationship and work on becoming whole, you will fill the hole.

I don't know what you may have experienced emotionally, but I do know that you no longer have to keep living it out. You can become whole if you desire to be. Ignoring your wounds won't make you stop hurting or make them go away. You will have to peel off the plaster you put over the wound and treat it. Confront your wounds, clean and treat them and let them heal. Do whatever you need to cleanse yourself from your emotional wounds and drop your baggage. It is time to become the emotionally whole wife God designed you to be.

A Clued-Up Wife in Waiting

There are certain quotes I find very unhelpful. Quotes such as "Ignorance is bliss" or "What you don't know won't hurt you." These two are especially unhelpful as they give the impression that a lack of knowledge is not a problem. I can tell you for a fact that it is. Ignorance isn't bliss, and what you don't know can hurt you, especially in the area of marriage. When you lack knowledge about marriage, you are setting yourself up for a lot of stress and pain in the future. Getting married without learning about marriage and your role in it is like driving a car without prior lessons. How do you know when to use the gears or press the brakes? How will you be able to tell the difference between the changing road signs? Without previous lessons, you are unlikely to get the car moving. If you do get the car moving, you are more likely to have an accident due to ignorance.

I know how it was for me when I first started learning to drive. I learned about the various levers and pedals and how they worked. By eighteen, I had my driving licence. By the way, I learned to drive while still at home in Nigeria. If you know my darling home country, you'd know that some areas of our society still need work. Driving and road safety is one of them. Now, imagine moving to the United Kingdom and trying to drive with my "Nigerian" knowledge. Let's just say I was clueless about some parts of driving because I had not been taught. I was also in a different country, so I had to learn the theory and practical aspects of driving all over again.

The same applies to your desire to get married. You must seek both theoretical and practical knowledge about marriage. There's so much to learn. You don't have to learn everything in one day, but you should learn something on your journey. The Bible has a lot to say about a kingdom marriage, and I would always recommend you start there. It is the one piece of knowledge that is true and can guide you in doing things God's way. For example, it talks about how a husband and wife should relate to their in-laws. Most challenges people face in this area can be sorted if they would only apply what the Bible says.

I learnt about in-laws before I got married. This doesn't mean that I haven't had my challenges, but I have always tried to follow what the Bible says on the matter. Has it always been easy? No, but I have knowledge that I try to apply as I go along. This is why learning about marriage is important, even during this season.

There are so many books about marriage, especially about kingdom ones. Find them. Set up a reading plan to learn from those with great marriages who have gone ahead of you. A great way to learn about godly marriages is to spend time with those with great marriages. Think of it as learning by observation. You don't even have to tell them that is what you are doing. You could hang out with them or offer to help them out with some house chores. I have found that people are more comfortable in their own space and will more likely be true to themselves. As you do this, pay attention to how they do life together.

I've given you a head start on what marriage is in the chapter on "Contracts and Covenants." Spend time seeking out more. As you do, you will begin to change your beliefs about marriage and your commitment to it. You will also be more intentional about who you want to make that kind of commitment to. When you know you are going into a covenant with someone, you will most likely make sure you don't choose the wrong person.

You should learn about the roles of both marriage partners. It's more than cooking food and paying bills. In some households, these roles aren't held by those who tradition would expect to, so don't get stuck on them. Instead, there are more profound roles. Roles such as helping your spouse fulfil God's purpose for their lives and being the head of the home. Think of it as learning about the gift you are to your husband. A gift he gets to unwrap every day till he dies, a gift he gets to be thankful for because you know your purpose in his life and are doing it. When you get engaged, you can work out who does what in the more superficial roles. At that time, I would recommend playing to each person's strengths.

If there is one thing you have been given in this season, it is the gift of time. Use it wisely so that your future self will thank you for it.

A Financially Fit Wife in Waiting

If there's one area I am glad I started to learn about on the journey to marriage, it is money. Money is a big deal, even though it shouldn't be, but it is what it is. Money has always had an impact on relationships. Never more so than the relationship between husband and wife. So, I would encourage you to learn about money in marriage. Learn how to manage money now as a single woman and how to manage it with another person. Money can be a real stressor in marriage. But, one of the best gifts you can give yourself and your future husband is knowing how to reduce the strain it can place on your relationship.

The best way to do it is to first get a biblical perspective of money. One thing you must know and settle is that God is the source of all wealth. Not your salary, investments, inheritance, gifts and all.

Everything belongs to Him and of His own, does He give us. You must never forget this. He can and will use people to bring wealth to you, but at the end of the day, it is all His.

The next thing to know is that He is the One who gives us the power to get wealth. He is the one who gives you ideas in business, leads you to the right job, and causes the works of your hands to prosper. It is not by your intelligence or hard work that you get wealth. After all, many hard-working people are poor.

The way money works in the kingdom is counter-cultural. The more we give away, the more we receive back. In the kingdom, when it comes to the wealth God has given us, we are custodians, not owners. That is why you must be willing to give when you are led to give. Generosity doesn't come with more wealth. It comes from a generous spirit that knows you are blessed and that there's more where that came from. So, in this season, learn to give with a generous heart.

When you resist giving or spending, you show your heart towards money. You likely need a heart check if you are always holding on to your money, whether from a place of fear or pride. Like I already said, you are a custodian, not an owner. Give when led, and be generous, seeking to bless wherever you find yourself. You must also be faithful with what you have, whether little or large. That means being faithful in your spending, saving and investing. Faithfulness unlocks even more wealth for you and requires greater responsibility. If you want to grow in wealth, be faithful with what you have.

This leads me to debt. You should owe no man anything except to love *(see Romans 13:8)*. It is not God's preference for you to be in debt. He would rather you be debt free and living within your means. It does not help to go into marriage with debt as it puts the marriage under unnecessary strain from the beginning. There's no need for that.

When it comes to money and marriage, there are some things you must settle. First, your money isn't your money. Remember, it is God's money in your custody. When you get married, what you earn is for the benefit of your unit, not only you. You become a unit when you get married. Your husband will be your head, and that includes being the head of your money. If he decides that he wants to spend the money in a certain way, you must be willing to submit to what he decides. This is why you should marry someone you are willing to submit and give your money to. You want someone responsible when it comes to monetary issues.

You must be ready to be open about what you earn, receive and have. Genesis 2:25 says they were naked and unashamed. Marriage, a good, kingdom marriage, requires vulnerability. For example, if you learned to hide money from your mother, then that is a limiting belief you need to deal with.

There are no set rules about managing your money in marriage, but here are a few tips.

Agree on how to cover your joint expenses, such as household bills and children's school fees. Ideally, both of you should have savings in case your family finances change in an instant. For example, someone loses their job, or unexpected bills arise. You might want to have spending thresholds on specific expenses. This gives autonomy but also allows for fewer money frictions.

Have a conversation about dependents such as elderly parents or siblings. There are usually cost implications for dependents. How these work out in marriage is down to individual situations. The key is to discuss what works best for both of you.

A good way to set yourself up with your money in this season is to **have good personal leadership**. This means knowing what you have and having a plan for your incomings and outgoings. You also want to think of your financial legacy. Remember that wealth in the kingdom is about stewardship and managing what you have well. Get clear on what you have. Know what is coming in and what is going out. This is the time to identify all your sources of income. Then determine what you spend.

Many financial experts recommend having a budget as it can help you get clear on your money. The main thing is to know if you are spending more than you are earning or receiving. If you are, this is the time to cut back and start living within your means. Marriage has enough stressors. Don't let how you spend money be one of them.

This is also a **time to save, invest and put money towards your retirement**. That is besides getting debt free if you are in debt. With debt, identify all that you owe and create a repayment plan. The experts recommend you start with the smallest amount and pay more than the minimum. You might need to call those you owe and set up a plan with them, and that includes family members. This is not something to be ashamed of. Think of your future and how happy you will be when you are debt free.

If you are in a place where you can save, invest and put money into a pension, do so. You can start with a little or a lot. It all depends on how much you have available. A lot of reputable support is available nowadays on how to do better with your finances. So, make an effort to seek out knowledge and become a woman who is an asset to her husband.

A Socially Savvy Wife in Waiting

I'll never forget a phrase I heard many years ago that gave me a good laugh at the time but also struck a chord with me. It was a series about relationships. The speaker mentioned that *"many Christians are so heavenly minded, that they are earthly irrelevant."* That phrase stood out. He went on to talk about how many Christians were so focused on heaven that they didn't fit into society. They didn't know how to relate to people without using "Christianese" language. For example, you'd greet a lady, and her response would be, "I am blessed and highly favoured."

Now, to each man, his own, but if you desire marriage these days, that kind of language may be off-putting for some. I know it was for me, and there are some people I know who would be uncomfortable with such language. The way I see it, we should be able to converse with everyone. Communication is a big part of what makes relationships work. It is also one of the first levels through which people connect. How do you talk to your closest friends or immediate family? That's the same way you want to talk to people you meet, especially on the journey to marriage. You want people, in this case, your husband, to see you and like talking to you. Speak as you would day-to-day. Be free and chat. This is not to say tell all your secrets but let the conversation flow. Do you catch my drift? This is how you build a friendship that may lead to marriage.

This brings me to something that I used to struggle with. Friendship, or should I say, my lack of male friends? When I first wanted to get married, there was usually a pattern in how things went. Girl meets boy; boy meets girl. Girl likes boy and boy likes girl. Then, they start a relationship and hope for the best. Nowhere in the societal roadmap to getting married are we taught how to be friends before dating. You do hear that couples should be friends with each other. Yet, you don't hear about being friends with someone and getting to know them before committing. Friendship is so important in marriage, but it starts before I do. The best marriages are where there is friendship and mutual respect. In this waiting season, one of the best ways to be a wife is to be friendly. I don't mean friendly with the ulterior motive of getting the other person to marry you. No, that isn't it. Be friendly because you want to know them for who they are.

Not every man you meet will be your husband. That's a fact. Some will be colleagues or business partners. Others may be connectors or even future husbands to your friends. Wouldn't it be sad to have missed out on having this because you viewed them only as a potential husband? When they didn't match up, you tossed them to the pile of could-have-beens. Learning to be friends with men you may meet will save you a lot of heartache. When a man is your friend rather than a potential husband, you can enjoy things without any entanglements.

As a single woman, I decided I wouldn't talk too long on the phone to anyone I wasn't committed to. I knew that long, drawn-out phone calls were a recipe for developed feelings for what may not be. This was the case when I met my husband; for months, we were just friends. I didn't put the relationship under any pressure. It was only after we both started feeling some tugs towards each other did we take the relationship further. Even then, we did our due diligence before getting into a relationship. We both knew we were going to marry each other before we started courting. More on that later.

I say all this to say, be friendly. In the same way, you may have different levels of friendship, have friendship levels with men. Friendliness is a good social skill to have. It makes people feel better around you but also makes your life richer. Not everyone will be a close friend. Some will be acquaintances; others may be friends with whom you can have a good time. You may not be able to confide in them about your deepest secrets, but you get on well. Some may be friends because of shared activities, e.g. work or volunteering, health and fitness. You should aim to have friends at various levels; recognise the place people take in your life.

Be friendly. Acknowledge people, smile when you see people or make eye contact. Start conversations and take time to hang out with people, especially those you would like to be friends with. Be genuine about your feelings towards people. Pay people genuine compliments. This is a skill that will make you attractive to your husband.

Hospitality matters and is a social skill that everyone should have. It is one of the ways people get to experience you. Your husband is probably looking out for this quality, even if he doesn't say it out loud. He is watching how you treat others and your disposition to hosting. Whether you know it or not, he is weighing you up against his qualities for a wife. You are also doing the same. That is how life is.

Since you won't live like a hermit, being hospitable is something you want to grow and develop now. You can learn it. It is not about having a big spread or loads of money. It is about serving people with what you have and how you make them feel comfortable. If someone comes to visit you, ask them how they got on and offer refreshments. When you visit, take a little gift. I encourage my clients to remember that they are intentional women. That includes being intentional about how people experience them.

The final thing I would say regarding social skills is manners. Mind your manners. Society may be losing its norms, but please don't join them. Mind how you speak to people, online and offline. We all spend a lot of our time online, but that doesn't mean we should forget our manners. Treat people how you would want them to treat you. Use your please's, thank you's, excuse me's, and I'm sorry's as required. Be respectful of people's time and yours too.

To become the woman who does these things, start today. Think of it as a trial run for where you are going. Remember, practice makes perfect.

A Physically Prepared Wife in Waiting

I have a friend who we call the Show Up queen. She believes that we all have something to offer the world, and we should show up with who we are and what we have. I have to agree with her and would be remiss if I didn't tell you about showing up as a woman who desires marriage.

A woman who shows up as herself is attractive. When I say she shows up as herself, I don't mean all made up and wearing the best clothes. Those things are nice, but it's much more than that. It is about being comfortable in your skin. It is about being true to your values in such a way that it exudes in the way you look physically. Let's be honest, men are visually stimulated. So the chances are that he will like what he sees before he steps toward you. The question I put to you is, "What will he see?"

I'll let you in on a "not so secret" secret - Your branding matters! How you appear will tell a man if you are the type of woman he is looking for or not. Certain men are attracted to certain women, and you have to ask why. It has to do with the message that a woman's brand is selling. What message is your brand selling? At this point, I want you to think about your physical appearance, manner of speech and even social media. What are they saying about you?

These days, social media and the internet gives people access to you. Companies can research you and determine if they want you on their team based on your social media. People have lost jobs because of what they put on their social media pages. This season is a great time to audit your social media. What is on your social media profile? What story is it telling? Does it tell the story of a woman who has evolved over the years? If you look at my social media page from when I first started to today, you will see a noticeable change. Your social media can attract or repel people from you.

Whilst we are on the topic of social media, you need to make your page accessible. What do I mean? Make it easy for people (ahem, men) to see and speak to you. Put a photo that clearly shows your beautiful face. Use your name, not a fake one. Check your message requests folder often. You never know who might have sent you a message. Many people have met and married their spouses this way. So don't stand in your way.

Social media is not the only way you can attract your future husband. Your looks also do the same. You must intentionally think about how you want to look. This is not to say you must wear a skirt or dress to attract your husband; far from it. But you should consider dressing in a way that flatters you, whether in the colours you wear or the styles you pick. As the daughter of a King, seek to honour God in how you look. As you do, He will honour you by giving you one of His sons who values what He does.

This is the time to think of your wardrobe, both inside and out. Let's start with your outer wardrobe. You want to make sure your wardrobe lines up with the kind of woman you are and the type of man you want to attract. As a godly wife in waiting, and I stress the godly, think of the kind of outfits in your wardrobe. Then consider whether they suit the woman you are becoming and the type of husband you want. What you wear says a lot about you, so think, what is your outfit saying? Does it say I am a classy, godly and graceful woman who wants a godly man or otherwise? This is not to say be drab in your dressing. You can leave loads to the imagination and look stunning at the same time.

Now to your inner wardrobe, and I am talking about your undergarments. Do you know how you seem to walk differently when you are wearing something that you look nice in? Well, your undergarments have the same effect. What you wear can bring you joy. This is not about sex but about dressing your body well. That starts with the first outfit against your skin. Choose undergarments that suit your body. That could involve doing things like a bra fitting, so you wear the right size for yourself. Choose colours and fabrics you like. If you have worn, torn and tired underwear, please bin it. Make it a regular practice to replace your underwear as often as possible.

As much as it is important to care about your wardrobe, it is more important to care about your body. Your body is the vessel you will use in your marriage and for childbearing. If you haven't started taking care of your body, this is the time to do so. Start by eating well. Be intentional about what goes into your mouth. This is not about dieting, but about eating so your body receives all the nutrients it needs to thrive. You want to be a healthy wife, and that doesn't start overnight when you get married. It starts now. What you make of your lifestyle now becomes your family's lifestyle in the future. Your children will learn to eat well if they see you eating well. They always model what they see.

You can also eat the right foods to prepare your body for pregnancy. Eating well should go hand in hand with some form of exercise. Find the activity you like doing and aim to do it at least three times a week. A little exercise is better than no exercise. Drink water as much as you can. Take your vitamins and supplements. Care for your skin, that is, your face and the rest of your body. Find products that support your skin and use them. Have regular medical check-ups. You want to know how healthy you are and if there are any adjustments you need to make to become healthier. After taking my program, a client of mine actually went and had a medical check-up. She wanted to make sure her reproductive system was healthy. After finding out one or two things, she acted on her doctor's recommendations. I remember her saying she didn't want to find out that she had any issues once she was married. As far as she was concerned, she would be on the back foot if that happened. That's a good mindset to have, as it shows you are preparing for what is to come.

Finally, you can focus on the activities society expects you to know as a wife in waiting. But to do that, I want you to understand the roles of husband and wife. There are some actions you can't swap when it comes to certain roles. For example, carrying a pregnancy, there are maternal instincts that a father can never have, no matter how much he tries and vice versa.

With that said, there are roles that society has prescribed to each sex. For example, the woman will keep and clean the home, whilst the man will bring home the money to pay the bills. There are usually unspoken expectations that the woman will be the primary caregiver while the man provides a supporting role in raising his children. But since this book has the Bible as its foundation, let us look at these roles as prescribed by the word of God.

First things first. Man and woman are equal in their creation. Therefore, when you stand before God, you are both equal. One is not superior to the other *(see Genesis 1: 27-28)*. Both man and woman are to do all God said in those verses.

Second, even though men and women are equal, their roles are unique and distinct. **Man** is to provide leadership and guidance to the woman and their children, and he is to provide for his family. Now, this doesn't mean the woman can't support him, but it is not her primary responsibility. **Woman**, on the other hand, is to help the man fulfil the role of leadership and guidance handed to him. She does this by running their home and making things easy so he can lead. Once again, this doesn't mean the woman should stay at home and never work, but her priority is family and home.

God made woman to help man *(see Genesis 2: 18)*. The word "help" in this verse is the Hebrew word "Ezer," which is also used in other parts of the Bible to describe the help God brings. As a woman, you are to come into the man's life, not as God but to provide help as God would. If your husband needs help, God has sent you and won't come to do what you are in his life to do. That is why He sent you to him. It is why your partnership with your husband must be purposeful. As a woman, your role is powerful and intentional, not accidental. If your husband is struggling, God's original design was that you would help him out of the struggle. That's the mindset you must have when you take on the role of wife. When you have this mindset, it is easier to slot into your place in your marriage.

So, now we know that the primary responsibility for running a home sits with the woman. One version of the Bible calls it being a manager of the household. A manager doesn't do all the work herself, but she has the ultimate responsibility for how things turn out. At the moment, you may be living at home with your parents, sharing with some friends or living on your own. Whatever setting you find yourself in, you should find ways to manage the household, whether food sourcing or meal preparation.

There are activities you can do right now that help you prepare for your future home. There are bills to pay, rooms to clean, laundry to wash and iron. The list goes on and on. If you currently live at home, take some of these and, going forward, make them your responsibility. Use it to train yourself on how to run your own home. If you live with friends or alone, these responsibilities are already yours. Be grateful for the practice.

Be A Wife

Now that you know what it is to be a wife seek to be one. Rather than look for a husband, strive to be a wife. Many will tell you different ways to attract your husband. But there's an easier way; simply be a wife! When Adam saw Eve, he was not confused about who she was. It was clear that she was everything he needed. The same can be true for you as a wife to your husband. When you are being a wife in waiting, your husband will recognise you.

Reflections

What did I already know that was affirmed in this chapter?

....

What new thing did I learn from this chapter?

....

What can I do with what I now know?

....

What example(s), if any, resonated with me and what didn't?

....

What have I learned that I can start doing right away?

....

Actions

Here are three things I will do based on what I learned in this chapter:

1. ....
....

2. ....
....

3. ....
....

"The similarity of values, goals and interests
will help you build a great relationship.
Opposites attract,
but commonality keeps them together."

12
A Kingdom Partnership

> The absence of a kingdom purpose for marriage makes it appear as if many couples have been married by the secretary of war rather than the justice of the peace.
> ~ *Dr Tony Evans* ~

From a young age, a lot of women dream of being married. Little girls set up their dolls, playing mummy and running their little doll houses. As they grow older, they seek the reality of their girlie dreams. They go into relationships looking for what they have dreamed of since they were little. Even when they have poor examples of marriage, a small part of them still hopes for a different story. As much as this is their desire, not every woman gets it right. Some do, others don't. Reading this book, I want you to be the one who gets it right. Your desire to get married is good but choosing any other way apart from God's is a recipe for disaster.

God's way leads to the right husband for you. His way, which is by the Spirit and with knowledge, takes you to the place of peace that your marriage should be. Nothing God does is by accident. Everything is intentional and purposeful. Choosing your husband and getting married must be the same. As a kingdom woman, who wants God's perfect will in marriage, you must have a clear picture of what that looks like. Having this clear picture makes it easier to be intentional and purposeful. So, let's start with the first part of the picture: *Your King Blueprint!*

Your King Blueprint

God never prepares you for preparing sake. Everything He does is purposeful. He won't prepare you for marriage, only for you to stay single. What would be the point of that? But you must know that preparing isn't all you need to do in this season of your life. Not only are you meant to work on your beliefs, embrace your identity and prepare for your marriage. You are also supposed to know the type of husband you should marry. Have you ever heard someone say, I missed the one for me because he got married? I have, and let me tell you something; it is not true!

Over many centuries, we have learned that the one exists. We have been told that there is only one person for us. If we lose them, that's the end. Many have been heartbroken because of this belief. In some cases, people have stayed single forever because of the one they lost. I beg to differ with this school of thought. I do not believe that there is only one person for you. I would go even further to say there are many for you. Yes, I know I am tampering with years of Hollywood scripting and church language but hear me out. There isn't only one person for you. You can meet many people, and if they fit "a type," you will have an excellent kingdom marriage with them. There is a template of the type of person you can be with, and many men can fit that template. I call it The King Blueprint.

The King Blueprint is the picture, template, or mould of the type of man you can be with. When God created you, He created you for a man. The blueprint describes the qualities of the man (your king) that you can be with. You need a certain type of man with you on your life journey. He must have a certain character, beliefs, purpose and spirituality. He will also have some compatible and complimentary extras. These are usually based on your likes, background and experiences. These extras draw you to him and him to you. A wife recognises her husband, just as a husband should recognise his wife. Any woman who desires marriage must have this picture of her husband. Now, I am not saying, take a physical picture of a man and put it up as your screensaver. I am saying that you must be able to recognise your husband when he shows up. If he is among your male friends, you should be able to pick him out from the crowd.

Not having a picture of the husband you want to marry is like trying to hit a target you cannot see. If you have no picture of the type of man you should be with, you will most likely not know when you meet him. That is why it is so important to have a King Blueprint. I always recommend it when I teach or talk to single women. Every woman who desires to get married must take the time to create one. It acts as a guide when you meet men and removes the confusion you might experience if you have more than one suitor.

Here's the challenge, though. Society, that big influencer, has told us that certain qualities are the right ones. If he has a place of his own, has a great job, and drives a nice car, then he has the makings of a good husband. It doesn't matter if he is also short-tempered and sees women as less equal to himself. What matters is that he can care for you and your children. Sound familiar? When you are waiting gracefully for your marriage, you will hear that no one is perfect. That is true, but you will also hear that you shouldn't set your standards so high. What they are saying is that you should manage what you get. But if you use society's checklist, it may be more than your heart that gets broken.

You may already have a checklist. Many of us know we need to have a list of what we want in a husband. But I have a few questions for you. What and who influenced your list? Is your list filled with qualities of a husband that will make your life easier? Did you write qualities that are a direct opposite of your father? Could it be that you wrote them because you don't want to end up with someone like him? If your checklist isn't true to who you are and where you are going in life, it is not a great checklist. Also, if you wrote the list without the Holy Spirit guiding you, you have short-changed yourself. He knows who is best for you and wants to guide you to him. Let Him help you.

When you are thinking of the man you want, here are some things to consider:

- I will live with him, day in, day out. I am not talking about living with him for some days or a few years. Think every single day for the rest of your life.
- I will raise children with him. If you don't like what you see or don't want to see the same character in your children, then you don't want to be with him.
- His family will become my family, and they will be in my life. You must pay attention to the family he came from. Even if he is a great, God-fearing man, you must be aware that his family will be yours too.
- His friends will be a big part of my life as they will influence him. So, if you like the kind of friends he has and the influence they have on him, then you are in a good place.

There are certain qualities your King Blueprint must have to make it a great blueprint. I have grouped them into three categories based on the level of importance. Not all qualities have the same level of impact on you and your marriage. For example, the fact that he is a good singer isn't as important as him being teachable. Some qualities are nice to have, while others are super important. When you're creating your King Blueprint, you must have this understanding. Start with the most important qualities and then work down to the less important ones. When I host a King Blueprint workshop, I help the attendees by colour coding the qualities. Green for the most important, yellow for the maybes and red for the no-nos. If you've never done this before, don't worry. The essence of this section is to help you create your blueprint. Let us start with the green qualities.

Green Qualities

The first and most important quality is a personal relationship with God. Yes, just like it is for you, it is of utmost importance for him to have a personal relationship too. His relationship with God is the most important quality you need in a husband. It is not the only one, but it is number one. A man that has a personal, growing relationship with God can be led, guided and chastised by God if need be. He may not be on the same spiritual level as you, but you must have similar beliefs. You may have heard the Bible verse, "Do not be unequally yoked with unbelievers, for what fellowship has righteousness with lawlessness, and what communion has light with darkness?" *(See 2 Corinthians 6:14)*. That verse is self-explanatory. As a woman who believes in God, His Son Jesus Christ and the Holy Spirit, you need someone who believes the same. It may not seem like a big deal when you are dating, but in marriage, it is. Life can and will happen in marriage. When it does, you want to know that the person you are with believes the same things you do.

Another green quality that should be on your blueprint is a good character. Character is what you will live with daily. Make sure that the one you want is worth living with. There are basic character qualities that you, your future husband and I should have. They are love, joy, peace, longsuffering, kindness, goodness, faithfulness, gentleness and self-control. Yes, those qualities that we all read about in Galatians 5:22-23. He should have them. They don't have to be a hundred per cent in him but let's start with fifty, okay? He will grow just like you are growing.

Other green qualities you need are common values, goals and interests. These are the bedrock of the best relationships. If you don't know what yours are, then you need to press the pause button on your blueprint creation. The word common means you already know yours and are looking for someone who has similar. Sit down and write out what your values, goals and interests are.

What is important to you?

What are your core values?

Where are you going in life?

What kind of career do you see yourself doing in the future?

What do you do for fun or enjoy doing to relax?

Knowing your values, goals, and interests makes it easy to recognise and connect with someone similar. The similarity of values, goals and interests will help you build a great relationship. Opposites attract, but commonality keeps them together.

You also want a man who is teachable and humble. Life expects us all to grow. A man who is proud or thinks he knows it all is less likely to grow. This is a recipe for pain and frustration and something you don't want to live with.

You also don't want to live with a man who cannot provide for you. Providing here doesn't mean he must have loads of cash but that he can take care of the family's basic needs. We are already settled on the man's role. You want a man that takes his role in the family seriously. I know we are in the twenty-first century, but don't forget that God wired men to be providers. Read Genesis 3 if you think I am wrong. God didn't have a conversation with the woman about work. That was between God and man. Now, I am not advocating for women to quit working. I love working and supporting women to work in the way they see best. But you must understand the qualities that matter if you want a kingdom marriage. Men are wired for work. That is why a man feels unsatisfied when he doesn't have work to do. If he doesn't feel unsatisfied without work, that signifies a problem. His work is important, and you want a man who sees it as so.

Yellow Qualities

Because you are not perfect, you must accept that your husband won't be either. He is bound to have minor flaws or imperfections. The question is, "Can you live with them or not?" These are your yellow qualities. I put these qualities here because they can swing in his favour or against him. Things like his accent, being untidy or disorganised. Or the fact that he turns up late to appointments or may not be open with his feelings. These are not bad things in themselves. But, it all depends on some factors. Does he have a growing personal relationship with God? Has he recognised his weakness? Is he willing or seeking to change when you tell him it upsets you? His attitude determines if these imperfections are deal breakers or not. Before you shut him out, remember that you have flaws too. People put up with your weaknesses and extend grace to you simply because they know you're not a bad person. With that said, here's how to recognise the yellow qualities that can go on your blueprint.

What imperfections or flaws can you tolerate?

What imperfections or flaws do you currently tolerate in others?

A good way to know what you can tolerate is to think of the things you accept from your loved ones at the moment. Those are your yellow qualities. Identify these qualities and add them to your King Blueprint.

Also in this group are your nice-to-have qualities. For example, do you want him to work in a particular place, be of a certain height or be from a specific tribe? Feel free to add them to your blueprint, as we all have things we like. There's nothing wrong with them; they most likely won't make or break you unless they have become idols. But I'm sure that's not the case.

Red Qualities
Some flaws are simply destructive. I call these the red qualities. You cannot and should not live with or accept them from anyone, including your king. These are character issues that can hurt and derail both you, him and your children. Such qualities include vile and vulgar words and behaviour, dishonest dealings and perverseness. Evil, lies, conceit, and pride are qualities you must be wary of. Is he deceitful, gets angry easily, lacks self-control, has addictions or is he faithless? You should give him a wide berth. Those are your deal breakers and MUST be in your King Blueprint. A man with these qualities has not mastered how to be a man of good character and reputation. He can only stand a chance with you if he acknowledges these flaws and seeks to be a better person. With that in mind, it's time to clarify your red qualities.

What flaws can you not live with?

What flaws are deal breakers, no matter how cute he seems?

What have been your deal breakers in the past, and do they still apply?

Note them down, and make sure you stick to them. I emphasise this because I know what can happen. When a woman has been waiting to get married for a while, it can sometimes be hard to stick to her standards. You might think you're being too strict and should ease up. Don't do it, sister. You deserve the right man, and your blueprint qualities will help you with that.

One Final Thing
Remember, your King Blueprint is a guide to help you recognise your husband when you meet him. When you finish creating your King Blueprint, put it in a visible place so you can see it often. What this does is help you cement the vision of your king in your mind. He becomes a living, breathing person because you know him so well. You see him all the time. This will not only help you

recognise him but also save you a lot of heartache in the future.

Marriage Mapping

The choice of a life partner can change everything for you. It will affect you emotionally, spiritually, financially, socially and mentally. Imagine he isn't paying the bills or helping you in the home. It could be cute short term, but what happens when it persists over many years? You will become bitter, emotionally down and financially out. A bad marriage can and will distract you from God's purpose for your life. It will cause you to focus all your attention on either trying to make it work or recovering from the wounds created. On the other hand, a good marriage can take you further into His purpose as you live a thriving life. Knowing which of these you want should guide your vision for your future marriage.

Having a vision for your marriage is important. Just as you need the King Blueprint, you also need a vision for your marriage. Proverbs 29 verse 18 (KJV) says, *"where there is no vision, the people perish: but he that keepeth the law, happy is he."* Vision ensures that you don't get things wrong. Even when things aren't going the way you would like, vision keeps you on track. You must have certain virtues in your marriage vision. These virtues must be more than romance and wanting to look good together for the 'gram. As nice as those may sound, they don't make a great marriage long-term.

When mapping out the kind of marriage you want, don't pattern it after someone you know. Instead, desire a kingdom marriage, a marriage that has its roots in the word of God. No one's marriage can be as good as the one God has for you. Your marriage has been tailor-made to you, so who better to ask than the One who wants the best for you? Let Him show you the kind of marriage He has for you. His Word has the qualities of a good marriage. You can't go wrong if you follow the Word of God.

If you are from a broken home, you must be even more intentional than others because your parents haven't given you a great vision of marriage. "*I don't want a marriage like my parents*" cannot be the foundation of your vision. God and His Word must be the foundation of your marriage vision. A desire for a kingdom marriage must be your driver.

One of the best definitions I have heard about a kingdom marriage is from Dr Tony Evans. He says, *"A kingdom marriage is defined as a covenantal union between a man and a woman who commit themselves to function in unison under divine authority in order to replicate God's image and expand His rule in the world through both their individual and joint callings."* Your marriage should be about making God known here on earth. All you've learnt is to help you know and live your calling or purpose. That way, it is easier to be intentional about who you can join up with to fulfil God's agenda. So, here are some of the virtues your kingdom marriage should have:

Unity
Independence
Transparency and vulnerability
Love
Friendship
Submission
Desire and a healthy sex life
Communication and connection
Humility
Gentleness
Bearing with one another
Forgiveness
Encouragement
Joy
Peace

Besides these virtues, you may have certain preferences. Do you want a specific number of children? No problem. Include it in your vision. Would you like a romantic partner? Feel free to pop that on too. Your preferences are just that; yours. There is nothing wrong with them, but you should filter them through the question "Why?" Asking why helps you check where your desire is coming from. Is it a good or bad place? You don't want your wishes to stand in the way of what God has planned for you. Trust me, you don't want to miss the marriage God has for you because you're holding on too tight to the wrong desire. That would be sad. As with your King Blueprint, you want to keep your Marriage Map in a prominent place. What you see often stays in your consciousness. Not only does it stay in your consciousness, but it also guides you as you get into your relationship. It helps you be and act as you should for the marriage you want. However, before you get into the relationship, it will guide you through your dating experience.

Dating Deliberately

Once you know the type of husband and marriage you want, you can start dating. Dating without these two in place is dating without intention. It is no different to going shopping for a dress without being clear on the style, colour or size you want. You'll either end up with no dress or get something you might not like in the long term. Your intention is important on your journey to marriage. It saves you a lot of guesswork and frustration. I am not a fan of the word dating, but it seems to be the firm favourite for what many people do, so I'll use it.

Dating is something created to allow people to test the waters to see if they want to swim. Personally, I think this is a waste of time and not the way God intended for us to experience the journey to marriage. Please hear me out. The way God intended for us to meet and marry is to be clear on who we need and then decide that someone fits that bill. He never intended for us to rush in and out of relationships in our search for "The One."

Anyway, back to dating. Dating is meant to be an intentional experience, and it can be. Take it from me. I have done both types of dating, society and God's. The bottom line is God's works. Hey! I am married after following His way, so I know it works. I want to share His way with you. Please don't shut down on me now. We've made it this far together and are almost over the finish line. This might be what you need to do differently to get the marriage you desire.

First, you shouldn't date until you are ready to. Society might scream at you to get into a relationship, but don't do it. Not until you are prepared for the experience, that is. Everything you've been reading and learning in this book is to help you get ready.

Here's a simple checklist you can use to check if you are ready.

Who am I?

What is God's purpose for my life?

Where am I going in life?

Have I or am I preparing for my marriage?

What type of husband do I need?

What type of marriage do I need?

You are good to go if you can confidently answer those questions. Couldn't answer them or are unsure of your answers? Take a breather and spend time learning more about those areas of your life. You want to be clear about these answers before you start dating. Dating without clarity in these areas will subject you to all sorts. From dating the wrong man to going with the flow in a relationship you shouldn't be in. Not worth it, I promise you.

Once you are ready, then it is time to date intentionally. Intentional dating is dating with a purpose and for the glory of God. The purpose of dating for you as a high-achieving, kingdom woman is to get married. That is the mindset you must adopt when you start doing it. You are not doing this only to see how things go. That is a waste of your time and not the way God wants you to do this. All the decisions you make and how you behave must be led by your purpose for dating. I am not saying you shouldn't have fun but don't forget why you are there. You want to get married, and there is nothing wrong with that. You can have male friends, go out and all because that is normal. You should be doing that. It's part of what helps you enjoy this single season of your life. All I ask is that when you decide to take things deeper, remember your why.

With that purpose in mind, I want to introduce you to **slow dating**. You may or may not have heard the term before, but slow dating is when you take your time to get to know the other person before you commit to them. With slow dating, you allow yourself time to see if this is the right person for you before committing to a relationship. I know this is a different way to do things, but I promise you that it is less painful. It gives you time to get to know the person without any exclusivity. Not only that, you save time as you don't end up investing time and resources in the wrong relationship.

When you practice slow dating, you can compare the man with your King Blueprint and see if he fits. If he does and wants to be in a serious relationship, you can choose to go ahead. I say *if he wants to be in a serious relationship* because you might meet someone who fits but isn't serious. Don't force it. If you are so convinced that he is the right person, speak to the Holy Spirit about it and let Him guide you.

When dating this way, every step is intentional. This means thinking in advance of what will make the dating experience pleasant for both of you. In the same way you have deal breakers in your King Blueprint, you should also have dating ones. So, what would constitute a bad date for you? He didn't bring you flowers doesn't count, by the way! I am laughing at myself here. I had read too many romance novels and thought a guy had to bring flowers to the date. So, imagine my shock and horror when my now husband didn't. Well, I am married to him today, which tells you that not bringing flowers wasn't exactly a deal breaker.

Jokes apart, what would make a good or bad date for you? Is it the way he is so touchy-feely on the first outing? Or is it that he never pays whenever you go out? Usually, whatever points to poor character would constitute a bad date. When people show you who they are, you should pay attention. If you go out a few times with a guy and notice a pattern, don't ignore it. Recognising what you don't want is easy when you know what you do want. So, prepare in advance. Be clear on what you want as part of your dating experience.

You can start things off on a light note. General conversations and outings in groups are the best places to start. This gives you the chance to observe and hear the person. People always show you who they are through their words and actions. One thing that is a must at the beginning of your intentional dating experience is that there should be no commitment. I know I said it already when I mentioned no exclusivity, but it bears repeating. No commitment allows you to speak to more than one person at a time. You can do this with honour and dignity because you are God's daughter. Your Father, through His Holy Spirit, will help you do it. Think of it as having many friends at a time, which you already have, so this is no different. You get to know different men over time with no exclusivity, and as time goes by, you get to know who you want to get close to. The whole essence of doing this is to prevent you from getting your feelings involved too early.

Dating is a good time to find out the kind of man he is and what he believes. Ask questions that matter. Don't only seek to know the size of his bank balance. Seek to know if he believes in God and what he believes about money as prescribed in the Bible. Ask what he thinks about current news and happenings in the world. You also want to know his background and how he grew up. Asking these questions helps you get to know him as a person, not only as a husband. Even as you ask questions, pay attention to how he acts. Our actions stem from our beliefs which guide our decisions and actions. Make sure that he isn't only talking the good talk but also walking the good walk.

Courtship

Only after getting to know him well enough should you move to courtship. At this point, you are committing to him for two reasons. First, he matches your King Blueprint, and you want to build a relationship for marriage. Courtship is building a relationship intending to get married. The keywords are "intending to get married." As kingdom women, we build a relationship for marriage. We are not in this for trial and error whilst hoping for the best.

You want to start the relationship by being clear about this. The relationship you are building with him is the beginning of your life together. At this point, you can have deeper conversations about money and previous sexual history. You want to share this kind of information with the person you are building your future with. In doing so, you allow them to know more about you and build honesty and trust. You are also making them aware of any responsibilities that may come with being with you and vice versa. For example, you have a child from a previous relationship or have student loans. They need to know this to know what they are getting into.

When you are courting, talk as much as you can. This is different from the dating phase, when you were getting a sense of the person. In this case, you are more aware and working to put together your future with him. This is when you talk about how to build a Christ-centred marriage. Topics like children, in-laws, careers and life goals must always be on the table. If you have any questions, you must ask them and be satisfied with the answers you get. A broken engagement is better than a divorce or miserable marriage. You want to build on the right foundation, so do your due diligence.

This is also the time to apply what you have learnt about building a good relationship. All the months and years of listening and learning about relationships aren't wasted. You have spent time reading books and practising with your nearest and dearest. The same way you do with them, do with him. Yes, there may be some finer details when it comes to your husband but remember that the principles for relationships are universal. You can apply the same principles with your husband as you would with your brother or friend.

How Do I Know If He Is The One?

How I wish I got paid each time I was asked this question. The number of times I have been asked, "Is this the person who will make me happy?" "Can I marry him?" In some cases, I have even been asked to confirm a choice. Well, sorry, sisters; not my place. I don't have a crystal ball (not that we dabble in that, anyways), and that just happens to be the Holy Spirit's department. By the way, He will only confirm God's desire for you. The Holy Spirit is only interested in God's will and desire, not yours. He only wants to reveal the heart of the Father to you. So, sorry to burst your bubble.

To help you make the right choice, start with your King Blueprint and Marriage Mapping (vision). Does he have the qualities you are looking for? Is the relationship like the one you want for your future? You want to answer yes to these questions. Marriage has its good and not-so-good days. Knowing that you are with the right person is a conviction you want to have for the more difficult ones. However, apart from your King Blueprint and Marriage Vision, you should also be clear on these other questions.

"Is this relationship drawing me closer to God or away from him?" The relationship God has for you won't pull you away from Him. It should draw you closer to God and help you grow. I am not saying you must pray and fast together every minute of the day; far from it. When it comes to that area of your relationship, you must find your rhythm as a couple. Remember that you are not copying someone else's relationship. You are looking for your unique relationship. This will help you not lose out because he isn't doing what your pastor does. Yes, I had to go there. Your husband isn't your pastor. Don't put that kind of pressure on him. What matters is that he has a growing relationship with God, and you can see the evidence in his life.

"Is he glorifying God in his personal life?" The man God wants you to be with must glorify God with his life. Once again, he doesn't have to be perfect in this area, but you should see that he is working on it. You want to be with someone seeking to glorify God in their life.

"What is the Holy Spirit saying?" You cannot ignore the place of the Holy Spirit when it comes to this question. You should always pay attention to the Holy Spirit so He can tell you if this is a go or not. While you're slow dating and courting, always ask the Holy Spirit what He thinks. If or when he proposes, don't get so carried away that you aren't paying attention to the Holy Spirit. Hopefully, before he pops the question, you will already know if he is the one for you or not. The Holy Spirit will tell you, if you are paying attention to Him, that is. So, keep asking Him and let Him guide you.

Accept God's Desires For You

Once again, the journey to a great kingdom marriage starts way before you say I do. It begins in this time of waiting gracefully.

This is your time to sit with the Holy Spirit; let Him paint God's desires on your heart. He doesn't want to override your desires but wants you to submit them to Him. Never forget that God's ways and thoughts are higher than ours. Whatever you think you want, His is way better. You cannot out-imagine Him. Trust Him and let Him lead you to the marriage He has for you.

Reflections

What did I already know that was affirmed in this chapter?

....

What new thing did I learn from this chapter?

....

What can I do with what I now know?

....

What example(s), if any, resonated with me and what didn't?

....

What have I learned that I can start doing right away?

....

Actions

Here are three things I will do based on what I learned in this chapter:

1..

....

2..

....

3..

....

"God has a great plan for your life and marriage, but how that happens lies in the choices and decisions you make."

13

From Promise to Manifestation

*"We have the seed of the gospel Word.
It is up to each of us to set the priorities and to do the things that make our soil good and our harvest plentiful."*
~ Dallin H Oaks ~

I don't share my story because I am perfect or have attained some level of perfection. I share it to encourage you, for you to see yourself in me and have hope. Sometimes it can feel like your journey to marriage isn't great, and others have it better than you. This may or may not be true, but this season is about you, not others. It is about the woman you are and the woman you can be. God isn't looking at you and demanding perfection for you to get married. He is not some puppet master sitting in heaven, looking to zap your every wrong deed. With a Father's heart, He is looking at you with only your best interests at heart. He wants you to become the woman that He knows you can be. He wants to set you up so you will thrive and manifest His plans and purpose when you get married.

This waiting season of your life is a gift, handed to you, all wrapped up. The choice to unwrap it is yours. Even when you unwrap it, the choice to use the gift is still yours. No one can force you to use it, but the truth is, if you don't, you have no one to blame but yourself. I don't say that to be mean, but it is the truth. If someone gives you something and you don't use it, you can't complain or blame the giver, can you?

This waiting season is a gift. It is a gift from your loving Father who wants to transform and prepare you for the next gift He has for you; your marriage! That is what this season is all about. It is a time to learn about where you are going and who you are. It is also about becoming the wife your marriage and husband need. God isn't in the business of bringing people together just for the sake of it. He is a God with eternity in mind. So, when He looks at you, He isn't seeing you as you are today. He sees you as He designed you to be; perfect! This season is to close the gap between who you are today and the woman He sees.

As the Holy Spirit led Jesus into the wilderness to be tempted by the devil, He has also led you into this season. Not to be tempted, although temptation will come but to become the woman He knows you can be. How do I know this? Because He's done it before; to the children of Israel when He was taking them to the promised land. God heard the children of Israel's cry for deliverance from the life of slavery they were living in Egypt. Not only did He deliver them, but He also promised to take them to a land flowing with milk and honey. Such a place like they had never experienced before. There was a shorter route to get there, but God, in His wisdom, said no. Instead, He took them through the wilderness. He took them through a longer route so they wouldn't turn tail when they saw war and return to their old life. He knew that there was a process they needed to go through to be able to take the land He had promised them.

As slaves, they weren't equipped for war or taking territory. The journey through the route that God had for them would change that. All they needed to do was follow and obey Him. God wanted to honour the promise He made to Abraham. But the nation He saved from Egypt was not fit for the promised land. The promised land hadn't changed since God made the promise, but the people weren't prepared. They needed to change their mentality from slaves to kings because only kings take over and rule territories.

He wants to do the same for you during your waiting season. He wants to take you from your Egypt to your Canaan, the promised land. Yet, it is so much more than your marriage. It is about taking you from the woman you are to the woman you should be in your marriage. A woman who is stripped and equipped in the wilderness so she can take territory when she gets married. One who is a king and priest who rules and reigns over her territory with God as her King. A woman who, as a result of the refining process she has been through, is multi-dimensional. First, a co-labourer with God making an impact in society. Then the wife and mother her husband and children need.

That is who God is calling you to be through this waiting season. There is no shortcut to becoming that woman, even if there is a shortcut to getting married. Oh yes! You can do various things to get married, but you cannot become that woman, the one God desires, by accident. She is a woman created in the waiting season through the refining she goes through. Unfortunately, so many women never meet her because of their perspective. To them, this waiting season (the wilderness) seems like an unending punishment. It looks so tough, so rather than go through the pain, they take the shorter route, rushing out to get into marriage. Well, we both know that the shorter route most often doesn't do what the longer route does.

The truth is we will all receive God's word about marriage at some point or the other. For someone, it may come as a stirring, a desire or a tiny flicker of hope. And for someone else, it may come through the picture you see of a couple who look blissfully happy. It might even come through the repeated questions of others on when you will get married. Yes, even those annoying questions could point you in the direction of what God has for you. God can use anyone and anything to get His message across to you.

Your Heart

When the promise, God's word on your marriage, comes calling, what will your response be? Your response will most likely depend on the type of heart you have at the time. The state of your heart matters so much as it not only determines how you respond to the promise. It also determines if you will step into the marriage God has for you. I wrote every word in this book to get your heart into the state God wants it to be. My desire is for you, as God's special girl, to become who He wants you to be. Of course, that's His biggest desire for you, but unfortunately, life can sometimes get in the way. All sorts happen in day-to-day life that can get to us. We process so much, and our hearts can take a bashing if we don't pay attention. So, as you will soon find out, the state of your heart can influence the woman you are.

In case you are wondering what I mean by your heart, I am talking about your internal processor. That inner place of emotions and passions, thoughts and decisions, character and self-will. It's the place that shapes who we are as people and the experiences we will live through. Whatever is going on in there determines a lot. It determines what we believe, who we believe and what we experience in life. Two scriptures that drive home this point are *Proverbs 4:23* and *Proverbs 23:7*. They both show that the state of your heart is vital to your daily life. Chapter four of Proverbs even takes it one step further by telling us to guard our hearts as it will affect all we are. Can you imagine that? The woman you are today and the one you will become depends on the state of your heart.

There are four states your heart can be in, but before I describe them and the way they shape the woman you are, please hear me out on this. I have been through each version in some shape or form. My heart has been bent out of sorts at different stages in my life, and I am still not perfect. I've been a **Rachel**, **Bella**, **Samantha** and **Apphia**. The names are to help us remember the attributes of each heart version; they are not actual people. Just thought I should put that out there before anyone comes for me.

I have finally evolved into the final version, but I can tell you that I am still being refined to become a better person. Daily, I try to be the woman God wants me to be because He never leaves anyone static, and He hasn't left me static. He will keep working on me till the day we meet in heaven, and I know He wants to do the same for you.

As you read about the different versions of the heart and see yourself in one or more of them, don't feel ashamed. We are all a work in progress. No one was born perfect, nor do we intentionally wake up and say we want to be a lower version of who we can be. At least I haven't met anyone who did. We are products of our upbringing, society, experiences and choices. Sometimes, we aren't aware that there is a better version of ourselves that we can be. So, we choose what we know and live as such.

If you see yourself in any of the versions I talk about, give yourself grace. You may be that version today; your heart may be in that state, but you don't have to stay that way. This book has given you what you need to become another version. I won't give away the secret of which version that is but believe me when I say, there's one you will desire. That version is God's version, and she is oh so beautiful! She is the version God wants you to be. As you become her in this waiting season, all you desire will come to you. Now, come along and meet our lovely ladies and decide for yourself which one you want to be.

Rachel

I shared something once on social media, and a lady commented about how it had helped her. Another lady replied, saying she should ignore what I said. Her exact words were, "leave the motivational talk to the motivational speaker." As I read this lady's comment, I wondered what had made her so cynical and why her heart seemed so hard. It wasn't only that she didn't see value in what I wrote, but she also didn't see why anyone else should.

Your heart can get to a place where you don't see value in what anyone offers, especially if what is being offered is spiritual. No one starts off that way, but it can happen. Life happens to us, and our hearts get a bashing. Even the softest of hearts can harden from the relentless cycle of disappointment, rejection and relationship pain. That lady's reply only revealed what was on her inside. Truth be told, her heart did not come across as very soft.

A woman with a Rachel-type heart is closed off and unable to receive what God has promised her in His word. Prophetic words and promises don't mean anything to her. Hopeful expectations about a marriage bounce off her when they are said or offered. When God makes a promise about marriage, a woman with such a heart disregards and dismisses it. She is cynical, shaped by culture, traditions, and her experiences. She believes there are other options than the ones God has to offer. A woman with such a heart will likely sneer at others for choosing to believe God's promise. The sad reality is that her life experiences and exposure to the ways of society have hardened her heart. She might not even know that her heart is that way because she has been like this for a while. You may hear her say, "Please, leave God out of this one." That's likely how those in her closest circle speak and think, so she is no different.

If you took the time to study a Rachel-type heart, you would see that it didn't start that way. Life experiences and exposure to societal traditions have shaped it. A woman with this type of heart would struggle to believe in God's promise when it comes. To do so would be to open up herself to potential disappointment, and she isn't willing to take that risk again. She has been there, done that and got the scars to show for it. So you can't blame her for closing off her heart. After all, no one wants to experience pain and disappointment.

The first way to tell a woman with a Rachel-type heart is by the state of her relationship with God. A woman with this type of heart may have no personal relationship with God even though she may go to church. I should know; I was this kind of woman for many years. She may also have had a relationship with God in the past but not anymore for whatever reason. Maybe she believed in God, and things didn't turn out as she expected, causing her to give up on Him. Now, this lack of relationship has had a knock-on effect. It has affected her beliefs, mindset, experiences and the people she interacts with.

For someone with a Rachel-type heart, change can only begin by connecting or reconnecting with God. That relationship influences everything else, including getting married. A relationship with God softens the heart, allowing it to hope and believe again. This is because He is the ultimate giver of hope. He is the one that helps us dream and believe again, especially when we have lost hope or are struggling to believe. For a woman with this type of heart, trying to become who God wants her to be can't happen without this relationship. She can try, but she will be a less-than-ideal version of who God wants her to be. That is why her relationship with God is the starting point. As she grows in Him, her heart melts. She becomes more hopeful as her faith grows. When the promise knocks on the door of her heart, her response will be, "This is possible."

You might be reading this and thinking, "Bunmi, you have just described me. I can see myself in Rachel. I've never had a relationship with God. When I hear the Word about marriage, I don't believe it is for me." Or it could be that you had a relationship with God but so much has happened to you over the years that you have given up on it. That's okay. All hope is not lost. You can connect with God and have a relationship with Him. He is waiting for you right now if you will reach out to Him. All you have to do is say, *"Lord Jesus, I invite you into my heart today. Come and be Lord of my life. I surrender my life to You from this day on, in Jesus' name, amen."*

If you have given your life to Christ in the past, your prayer is a bit different. The reason is that Jesus never left you even though you stopped acknowledging Him. His Spirit was always there because He promised never to leave or forsake you. He is in you and wants to relate with you. So your prayer is, *"Holy Spirit, I acknowledge that you are with me and in me. I want us to have a close relationship. Help me to know You more, in Jesus' name, amen."*

As you begin the journey of growing your relationship with God, things will start to change in your heart. This will, in turn, affect the experiences you have. Trust me when I say it is the best relationship you can invest in.

Bella

Have you ever met someone who was always excited about some great idea or product they had, yet when you spoke to them a while later, they had lost that excitement? Well, I have; both met and been that person. They most likely started working on the idea but gave up along the way. If you've met someone like that or are that person, did you take time to think or even ask, what happened? I did. Guess what happened? They, and I, encountered the *in-between*. That's the place between idea and success. It's that place where a lot of dreams and ideas die. It is where our character develops, growth happens, and we need a heavy dose of discipline and diligence to push through.

It is also the same place where a woman with a Bella-type heart is revealed. How do you know a woman with this type of heart? You know her by what she does when the excitement has faded, and the rubber hits the road. A woman with this type of heart receives the promise with excitement. The promise may have come as a prophetic word or during her quiet time with God. Whichever way, she received it with excitement. But as weeks, months and maybe even years rolled by, without seeing the fulfilment of that promise, she began to lose heart and, in some cases, was even offended with God.

Yet, she is not like her sister with a Rachel-type heart. A woman with a Bella-type heart has a relationship with God, but it is rather shallow. I would even go as far as to say she is religious, and most of what she knows of God is what others have told her. She knows what others say about God because she attends church services and does religious activities. Yet she has not spent time growing her roots in Him through a personal relationship. This has affected her ability to be resilient and have staying power. For this type of woman, her view of God may be clouded by her experience with her natural father or what people say of God.

A woman with this type of heart hasn't learnt how to take God's promise from a word she knows to her reality. As time goes by and nothing seems to happen, she may decide that maybe she isn't meant to get married. In her heart, she may think the promise wasn't for her or that there are other alternatives. In time, she ditches God's promise and settles for an available alternative. Remember the detours I talked about a few chapters back? She will likely go down a few as she considers other options to get what she desires. Even though she wants the companionship that comes with marriage, she may seek it in other ways.

For a woman with a Bella-type heart, this waiting season is the time to grow her roots in God. It must be her highest priority as she needs to get to know God for herself, not through what others tell her. She needs to know His ways if she wants to keep the promise alive and see its manifestation. She needs to understand that God is the One who gives the power to keep going when things aren't happening as quickly as we expect. I would even recommend she asks God for some encounters that birth conviction. When I say encounters, I am not talking of angels and demons or any of that stuff. I am talking about experiences that will convince her that God is real and interested in her; experiences that will help her know God in diverse ways and grow her faith. The convictions she builds will keep her going on the days when it looks like nothing is happening.

I don't know what your journey has been like, but if Bella reminds you of yourself, don't fret or feel bad. God is inviting you to get intimate with Him. He is inviting you to that place of closeness and personal encounters. He is holding His hand out to you, saying, *"Come, I want to make Myself real to you."* As you do so, He will begin to show you all that you need to become who He wants you to be. So even when the doubts arise, which they will, you won't be overcome by doubt. You will understand that doubting God doesn't mean you have failed as a Christian. It is just your humanity shining through, and that's fine.

Samantha
Distraction never lets you get to your final destination. That's what I have realised, but a woman with a Samantha-type heart may not

know this yet. She is different to Rachel and Bella because she does have an established relationship with God. Her challenge is that she is distracted by the many shiny objects which catch her attention. It is not that she wants to be distracted. She wants to get married, but her attention is being pulled in different directions.

I'll be honest, getting distracted on this waiting-for-marriage journey is very easy because there's so much on life's journey to take your gaze off God's promise. So, don't knock a woman with a Samantha-type heart. Life happens. Your biological clock keeps ticking, and your friends are getting married. Then your family are asking you when you will bring someone home. And we aren't even adding in all the photos with #couplegoals on Instagram. The list goes on and on, and if care isn't taken, reacting to them can become a distraction from what God wants for you.

The problem with distractions is that they take your gaze off the promise, and in time, they will cause you to lose sight of it altogether. In doing this, you begin to focus on what is not so important and start looking at what is happening to others. This is where the comparison game begins, and the feeling of being left behind kicks in. Without even intending to, you start to resent God for what isn't happening. You feel that God is unfair because He is giving "*them*" what you desire, and it seems He's forgotten all about you. It's a distraction you don't need as it will ultimately derail you.

Distractions are powerful like that and can take you down a rabbit hole you never intended to go down. This is why keeping God's promise about your marriage before your eyes is so important. When you see the word God has given you daily, you are less likely to get distracted. Doing so will help you take conscious steps toward the promise as faith rises within you. Oh, keeping the word in your consciousness will grow your faith.

At this point, I would love you to take some time to reflect on Samantha and ask if this is you. There's nothing wrong with admitting it. To acknowledge where you are is always the first step toward change. The toughest part of any change is accepting that you need to change. When you don't acknowledge your distractions, it will be hard to see that you have lost sight of what is important; God's promise to you.

If you feel that I have just described your heart, I want you to know that you can refocus on what you desire, and hopefully, reading this can help. Take God's promise to you and keep focusing on what is important on your journey to marriage. It is time to become that woman who stays focused on where she is going. You will stay on track when you keep what is important before you. Having a focus helps overcome distractions. Focus will help you see what is important and what you need to get there, dropping all that's unnecessary by the wayside.

Apphia

After reading about these women, you may think that the woman for your marriage is unattainable. She seems to be some perfect, holier-than-thou sister who never did anything wrong. If that were true, people like you and me would never match up. I was and still am not perfect. God is not looking for a perfect woman. No, He is looking for a woman who seeks to know Him and herself. A woman who is constantly maturing into the woman she believes God has called her to be.

It is that woman that this whole waiting season is about. That ever-maturing, God-focused woman who wants to be all God has created her to be. She is the woman who hears the promise, believes it and holds on until it comes to pass. How does she do this? By growing her relationship with God and evolving into who she is destined to be. As she does so, she becomes a woman with an Apphia-type heart. By the way, Apphia is a name that means fruitful.

To be a woman with an Apphia-type heart is not about being a hundred per cent perfect. Like I already said, God isn't looking for perfection. If He were, none of us would ever match up. Even at thirty per cent, a woman with an Apphia-type heart is getting results because she is fruitful. She is growing and maturing into who she is meant to be. She attracts the right experiences and people into her life because she is growing. If that is happening at thirty per cent, imagine what will happen as she grows to forty or seventy per cent.

First, the not-so-secret weapon of the woman with an Apphia-type heart is her relationship with God. The more she submits herself to God, the more she becomes who God designed her to be. I am the woman I am today only because of my relationship with God. I started taking my relationship with God seriously at some point on the journey, and it changed me. This is not only true for me but for many other women that I know. I have interacted with many women from all walks of life, and one common thread in fruitful women is God. I am not talking about significant career milestones and high-priced items kind of fruitful. Those things are great, but I mean the kind of fruitful where all areas of your life are thriving.

When I teach, I tell people that a relationship with God is the foundation upon which you build everything. So, if you are struggling to believe the promise, check your relationship with Him. He is the promise; the marriage He promises you is a benefit you get from getting Him. As you focus on Him, His word and His ways, faith will rise in your heart. It is this faith that helps you believe and keep going on the journey. If you have desired to change but have faltered, start by looking at your relationship with God. A relationship with God is the power that charges every other aspect of your life.

Another trait of a woman with an Apphia-type heart is that she is teachable. Every time you meet her, she seems to have grown a bit or a lot more than the last time. She is never static. Not only that, but she is also humble enough to acknowledge when she needs help or doesn't know something. She is willing and seeking to learn all she needs to become the woman she is meant to be. She knows that this is what will bring the promise she has received for her marriage to pass.

For a woman with an Apphia-type heart, the goal is not to be perfect but to keep growing. The key word is growing. Each day is an opportunity to become better, wiser and more aligned with the woman God is building. That means that even when she falls, she picks herself up and continues the journey. If she notices traces of Rachel, Bella or Samantha, she makes the needed correction. Then she continues keeping her heart in a state that allows her to grow and be fruitful. So, even though some traces of the other heart types may be found in this woman, they are not dominant. What is more dominant is a heart that seeks God, a heart that is teachable and continually maturing.

Align Your Heart With God's

As I said before, these heart types are not meant to make you feel bad about who you are right now; far from it. Describing these heart types is intended to help you on your journey. To give you a vision to strive for. The state of your heart determines who you are and what you get in life. Your heart is vital to getting the marriage you desire and the one God has for you.

I should mention that even though a society-defined marriage is in no way the same as a God-defined marriage, God can align the kind of marriage you want with the one He has for you if you have the right type of heart. I find this so amazing and encouraging because it shows God's heart towards us, His daughters. When He aligns your heart with His, you desire both the kind of marriage and husband He wants for you. Now, that sounds like the perfect will of God and, my dear sister, nothing can beat that!

The Promise Is Here

It was the morning of my wedding. I was alone in my hotel room, which is a rarity on a wedding morning, especially as a Nigerian. Usually, someone would have slept in the same bedroom with you, and you would wake up to a hive of activity. But this morning, that was not the case, and I know God did it for a reason. I believe He wanted us to have our moment before everything took off. As I basked in that moment with Him, my phone went off. A friend of mine had sent me a message congratulating me on the pending wedding. She sent me a song that spoke to my heart that morning. It was Sinach's *"He did it again."* It captured my heart towards God that morning because I had woken up so grateful. Grateful for what He had done over the years to get me to that point. He had done many things and given me so many experiences. As I sat there all alone, I was so grateful. God was doing it again, doing what He had promised He would do.

The waiting gracefully journey I had been on for many years had brought me to this point. I had not arrived at this point by accident but by grace. Remember how I introduced grace at the start of this book? It is the power of God that reaches down to humanity for humanity's sake. As I soaked in the words of the song, gratitude kept flowing through me. God gave me solitude that morning, so He and I could have our special moment before I walked down the aisle. That is something I will always be grateful for.

As I said my wedding vows later that afternoon, I said them not as the Bunmi who met her ex-fiancé eleven years before. That Bunmi was long gone. I was now the Bunmi God had always intended me to be on my wedding day. This was the Bunmi the journey of waiting had shaped. She was wiser and more mature than the girl who started the journey. For one, she didn't nitpick on every single wedding day detail. Trust me, as someone who usually wants to know all the details, that was a big sign of how I had matured.

I was more focused on getting married than the wedding, much to the frustration of my wedding planner. It wasn't that the wedding wasn't important to me, but my marriage was far more important in the grand scheme of things. The wedding was only one day, but my marriage was going to be for years, by the grace of God. In the latter years of waiting, I spent more time thinking about my marriage than my wedding day. That shift in mindset only came as I waited gracefully, and the most important things became clear.

Please hear me; I am not saying you shouldn't think about the type of wedding you want. Of course, you should, but it is more important to dwell on the kind of marriage you want. When the party is over, and all have left, that is what you will have, so make sure you like what you have. When it is only you and your husband, you want to be sure that the marriage you will be living in is what you want. So what kind of marriage would you like?

In case it wasn't clear in the previous pages, let me say this: God knows the kind of marriage you should be living in, so ask Him to show it to you. Ask Him to give you a desire for it so strong that you do everything to get it. When I say everything, I mean all you have learned so far and need to do. His grace is more than enough to help you.

As much as this book focuses on marriage, your waiting season is not about marriage alone. Think of your desire for marriage as an invitation. An invitation to a party, where the guest of honour is you. A party where the entire set-up is for you to meet you, the you that your future awaits and deserves. The you that your husband and children need. The you that God will say to, *"Well done good and faithful servant. You were faithful in your waiting season, and now you have the results to show for it."*

At a time when morality is at an all-time low, and there is a shortcut for everything, waiting gracefully can seem like a waste of time. What's the point of following such a journey with high standards when others aren't? After all, some people get the marriage you desire without following such a path. Why must you follow this path where it seems like *"your own is too much,"* as they say in my home country? Simple; because what you get at the end of the journey is worth it. Let the world think whatever they want of you. That's their business, not yours. What you desire, the marriage God has for you requires your own to be too much, which is okay. God-grade things aren't acquired by doing what everyone else is doing. You will have to follow the road less travelled by the crowd. Some might even mock you for choosing such a path, especially if things don't pan out immediately. Please don't let that put you off. This path, the one of waiting gracefully, is so worth it in the end.

As you become who God designed you to be and equip yourself for your marriage, you will attract your husband. Not only that, but your experience will also be richer and fuller. That's something that no one can give to you but you. So, are you ready and willing to wait gracefully?

Reflections

What did I already know that was affirmed in this chapter?

....

What new thing did I learn from this chapter?

....

What can I do with what I now know?

....

What example(s), if any, resonated with me and what didn't?

....

What have I learned that I can start doing right away?

....

Actions

Here are three things I will do based on what I learned in this chapter:

1..
....
2..
....
3..
....

"God didn't make a mistake when He made you.
You are His child,
and He would do anything for you.
Even when you mess up, He still loves you
and will always love you."

About the Author

Bunmi Oduah is a relationship expert and teacher who is passionate about helping women find joy in being single whilst waiting to get married. After a decade-long career as an environmental regulator, she traded her personal protective equipment for jeans and pretty tops and turned to helping women who wanted to get married. She has always been passionate about relationships, even writing short love stories as a teenager. Today, she helps women write their love stories.

When she isn't teaching about waiting for marriage and relationships in her digital programs, she can be found spending time with her husband and two children or having soul-stirring conversations with her friends. To learn more about Bunmi and working with her, visit www.bunmioduah.com.

www.ingramcontent.com/pod-product-compliance
Lightning Source LLC
Chambersburg PA
CBHW032223080426
42735CB00008B/687